OBSERVATIONS

ON OUR

INDIAN ADMINISTRATION,

CIVIL AND MILITARY

OBSERVATIONS

ON OUR

INDIAN ADMINISTRATION,

CIVIL AND MILITARY.

BY

LIEUT-COLONEL JAMES CAULFIELD, C. B.

GYAN

Published by

Gyan Publishing House
5, Ansari Road
Daryaganj, New Delhi-110002
Phone: 011-47034999, 9811692060
E-mail: books@gyanbooks.com

Distribution Network
gyanbooks.com
India, USA, Canada, UK, Australia, France

ISBN: 978-81-212-8034-1 (PB)
First Published, 1831

2nd Impression 2023

Printed at: Gyan Press, Delhi.

OBSERVATIONS ON OUR INDIAN ADMINISTRATION, CIVIL AND MILITARY
Author: JAMES CAULFIELD

OBSERVATIONS

ON OUR

INDIAN ADMINISTRATION,

CIVIL AND MILITARY.

BY

LIEUT-COLONEL JAMES CAULFIELD, C. B.

OF THE BENGAL ARMY.

LONDON:

SMITH, ELDER, AND CO, CORNHILL,

1832.

PREFACE.

In submitting the following observations to the notice of the public, I must disclaim every motive but that of drawing attention to the situation of our Indian Empire; the stability of which is inseparable from the interests of our country. I have endeavoured to preserve my mind uninfluenced by personal views. Whatever they may be, I am frigidly indifferent as to the effect this work may have in facilitating, or retarding them. It has been my anxious desire to avoid bias towards any received opinion, or being influenced by any party. I have served long in India, and have been employed in many branches of the Government, and have had the honour of gaining its approbation. I now, with feelings of deference, lay before my countrymen, such observations upon the several departments of our Indian administration, as appear, in some degree, to merit the regard of every man solicitous about the public weal.

Note.—*These Observations were sent home from India in November 1829, for publication; but from circumstances beyond the Author's control were not published.*

CONTENTS.

OBSERVATIONS,

&c. &c.

POLITICAL.

WHETHER the existing government be the best that can be devised, and is calculated to secure the greatest benefit to England and India, or whether it is capable of improvement, and if so, in what manner, are serious questions, upon which few, even of the best informed, think alike, and demand the deliberate and mature consideration of the legislature and people of the United Kingdom.

In the contemplation of a question of such deep importance, involving the happiness of many millions of people, and the best interests of our country; every selfish or interested feeling ought, as far as our nature will admit, to be laid aside, and our minds brought to a subject pregnant with good and evil, free from prejudice, and with the least possible bias. The discussion of this question should not be hampered with theories; every thing should give way to the result of experience, and the wholesome test of truth.

This investigation, whenever it may take place,

should be carried on with a patient and diligent scrutiny into every department of the government. Political, judicial, territorial, commercial and military, should each be thoroughly sifted, and, if necessary, revised; but as this division of the subject is unconnected with the matter immediately before us, we shall leave it for the present, and revert to the question; whether, at the expiration of the charter, India and its government, as they now stand, should be continued to the Honorable the East India Company, or whether the Crown should resume the immediate charge of the vast empire that the valour, the wisdom, and energy of the nation has achieved in the East? The glory of England, and the continuance of our dominion in Europe, Asia, and Africa, would appear to rest upon the result of the decision; and every nation of the earth will await with intense anxiety, and deep interest, the opinion which parliament, when called on, shall pronounce upon this vitally important question; and no doubt the united wisdom of the nation will ponder seriously, before it hazards an opinion upon a subject on which the liberty of England, and the existence of her colonies depend. The most daring innovator will pause before he advises a change in the construction of a vast and complicated machine that answers so well the purpose for which it was constructed; more especially when he reflects that the slightest omission, the most trivial oversight, may serve to create a monstrous power in the hands of a minister, who may, or may not, be a good and wise man; consequently such a power would be liable to be wielded to the destruction of that constitution which has long been the boast of England, the palladium of liberty, and the dread of despotism.

When this immense question is brought before the public, advertence will, no doubt, take place to the discussions in parliament upon Mr. Fox's India Bill, which will serve to call the attention of gentlemen to the imperious necessity of keeping out of the minister's hands the means of retaining possession of his place when the measures have ceased to be beneficial to the nation. It should never be forgotten that gold will tell upon the necessities of the highest; human nature is, and must continue defective; and wisdom will, in legislating for the future, keep a strict eye upon the infirmities to which mankind have ever been liable. It is not sufficient that parliament is pure; precautions for preventing the application of means calculated to corrupt its integrity must be adopted, which will necessarily point out the salutary effects that might be expected from a partial revision of the Indian departments in England. It cannot be denied that the Board of Commissioners for Indian affairs absorb the whole of the executive authority, leaving the Directors a powerless, and worse than useless body, possessing sufficient nominal authority to enable His Majesty's ministers to saddle them with the mismanagement and odium caused by the superordinate body. While the Governor-general and the members of government can be recalled by the crown, and no governor appointed of whom His Majesty's ministers do not approve, who can assert that parliamentary influence will not operate on our governors, who are virtually dependent upon the minister, or that such a state of things will not secure a powerful and predominant weight with those members of parliament who have sons, brothers, and other near relations in the Company's service? The principle that conduces to this evil will induce the minister to lend all his interest to screen a Governor-general who is actually the creature of his power, and dependent upon his will. If the pernicious effects of the controlling Board, under the positive dictation of the cabinet, requires illustration, we shall find in the conduct of the Board in 1785, the year after its creation, with regard to the settlement of the Nuwab of Arcot's debts, ample proof of the injustice, disgrace, and pollution which was the result of the establishment of a power, alike inimical to the true interest and honour of England, and her Asiatic possessions. Let Paul Benfield, and his attorney, Atkinson, serve as an illustration and a warning of the contamination and infamy that may be introduced into our House of Commons, through the means of an interference with our Indian government. Let this serve as a beacon for future ages, to avoid "the golden cup of abominations; the chalice of the fornications of rapine, injury and oppression, which was held out by the gorgeous eastern harlot, which so many of the people, so many of the nobles of this land, have drained to the very dregs." Experience has proved, that the executive functions can never be salutarily exercised by the supreme authority of the nation. Our Indian government should be effective and responsible, whether it remains in the Company's hands, or is transferred to the Crown; and if it be continued to the former, the Governor-general should be selected by the court, under such restrictions as would ensure an impartial choice. He should not be drawn from their service; his fortune should be unimpaired; and he should be confessedly a man of talents and experience. In legislating for our Indian possessions, it should be recollected, that Mr. Pitt introduced his celebrated bill as a palliative, rather than a remedy for the evils then existing in the government. In framing rules, therefore, for our Indian empire, it appears essentially, if not imperatively necessary, that its altered state and condition should be thoroughly ascertained, and fully understood, and that the chances and changes to which it is exposed should be calculated on, and provided for, to the utmost extent of human foresight and prudence. The period is rapidly drawing near, when the charter, under which the present system exists, will expire, and the awful question, how our distant realms are to be governed for the future, will force itself upon the deliberation of Parliament, and the nation. Our sway in Asia is no longer a subject about which the country can be indifferent; the interests of England have become inseparably interwoven with the welfare and security of our Asiatic sovereignty, which has gradually, imperceptibly, but naturally, forced itself into contact with one of the most powerful nations in Europe. In the present state of things it must be manifest to the most desultory observation, that England, and Russia, must either guarantee the independence of Persia, or the former must look on with unwise, and incomprehensible indifference, whilst the latter establishes her influence, if not her dominion, over that state, and gains a position, that will secure an easy entrance into our Indian territories.

Russia, immense, extensive, and powerful as she is, has not yet reached the fulness of that gigantic size, at which fate has apparently destined her to arrive. Upon her southern, and eastern frontier, the countries of Khorasan, and Bucharia (the latter of which, is under the influence of petty, but turbulent, and warlike chiefs) present by no means a difficult nor insurmountable barrier to the attainment of an influence, that may be exerted to our serious detriment if not to our imminent danger. Hordes from independent Tartary, little Bucharia, and Thibet, would gladly join under such powerful auspices, in a plundering excursion into India. It will be wise to recollect, that our immediate eastern frontier, has already become insecure; a provident and cautious policy will instruct those who preside over the destiny of our Indian empire, to adopt such measures, as wisdom may consider best calculated to embrace and provide for all contingencies.

The vast and profound problem of government is susceptible of so many, and varied solutions, as to puzzle the most vigorous, comprehensive, and discriminating capacity; therefore the less complicated it is, the better. A simple piece of machinery, must obviously require fewer repairs, be exposed to fewer accidents, and when out of order, be more easily restored to its functions, and at less hazard, and expense, than a more intricately constructed instrument. The more, therefore, our system of government is simplified, the less exposed it becomes to danger. Colonies are supposed better provided for by a simple form of polity, than when subjected to numerous and conflicting regulations. To secure to any distant country an equitable, energetic, and efficient government; we have only to guard against a minute interference with the natural genius of its inhabitants; render their lives and properties secure, and allow them a just and adequate share in the executive government of the state. In other words, identify the interests of the population, with those of the ruling authority; and allow active and honest industry a fair and legitimate competition.

When the rights of the community are not respected and secured, there cannot possibly exist a sound and affectionate devotion; there must be a reciprocal conviction, that each is necessary to the prosperity of the other: without such an impression, there can be no union of interests, no common cause to rally round, nor common principle to impel: So long as the rights of the bulk of the inhabitants are made subservient or are sacrificed to the aggrandizement of the few; so long will injustice, dissatisfaction, and a desire to change the existing system disturb the community.

To render a foreign possession secure, we must obtain some hold in the soil, which, in a country in a great measure occupied, can only be accomplished by cautious and slow degrees. The governed and governors, to render the one happy, and the other stable, must have a community of feeling upon all important subjects; they must assimilate in religion, usages, manners, language, and education; every thing tending to accelerate such a consummation should be encouraged, and every thing disposed to retard it should be removed with prudence, or guarded against with undeviating solicitude. Hence it is clear, that colonization, under limited restrictions, should be admitted, and unless this necessary step be taken, our footing in India must continue infirm, and exposed to every commotion which may agitate the public mind. The security of our possessions, the prosperity, peace, and good order of society, alike demand that we should take a liberal and extensive view of our situation. It is time to cast off the trammels which have bound us, and extricate our minds from the bugbears which have hitherto prevented our making the slightest advance towards securing ourselves in that distant land. After occupying India for the best part of a century, we may look round in vain for a class, upon which the several important duties in the various departments of the executive government could devolve, without ruin being the consequence. We are informed by an able and philosophic historian, Mill, that, the most experienced of the Company's judicial servants are unanimous in the opinion that, the * zumeendars and merchants, are alike unfit for any confidential employment in the executive branch of the government, nay, that their employment would prove mischievous, consequently it would not be advisable that they should be invested with any judicial authority, because such an investiture would entail innumerable evils upon the people. There are none to feel sentiments of regard and respect for the government, and yet be bound to the people by a common interest, and sympathies growing out of a daily, intimate, and social intercourse; the state of society is fictitious, and disjointed. There exist none, who, in the hour of danger, would exert themselves to aid the executive authority; such a class is unknown, and without it permanent stability is not to be attained. Government, in its present isolated situation, can neither ascertain the wishes nor opinions of the people,

* Landholders.

nor explain fully, matters of which it is necessary they should have a thorough knowledge. In the face of such opinions, held and proclaimed by our ablest servants; in the face of prolonged experience, and in defiance of common sense, are we to continue bound in the chains of selfish avarice, and besotted prejudice? We cannot now plead ignorance, and the necessity of experience; the first has ceased to exist, the latter stands copiously recorded in the every-day transactions of our rule.

This class in our Indian society, would appear to be our chief want; it also appears that through its influence alone, we can entertain any rational hope of perpetuating our dominion. By taking root in the soil, and thoroughly incorporating ourselves with the inhabitants, we shall succeed in becoming a part of the population, and creating a communion and identity essential to our existence; without which our dominion cannot be considered as established upon a permanent foundation. The history of India, from the period when we were first called upon to take an active part in its affairs, has, down to the present moment, satisfactorily and incontestibly proved that we cannot avoid doing so, in every question that arises between the states with which we are connected. The opinion entertained by some of the leading men in Europe, "that by a steady and conciliating conduct, the lasting tranquillity of our eastern possessions might be secured," is a mere chimera, tending to precipitate our downfall, unless it be supported by a population, actuated by a community of feeling, a similarity of manners, reciprocal advantage, and a conviction, that the prosperity of the one, rests exclusively upon the safety of the other. A religious impostor of either sect is at present able to agitate and inflame the public mind, from one end of India to the other. This is not an assertion unsupported by facts. Let those who observe and reflect on passing events attest the verity, or prove the fallacy, of the supposed danger attending religious imposition, combined with any political feeling inimical to our interest in a country, where superstition, and a passive and blind obedience to their spiritual guides reigns triumphant over a population of millions, a population from whence the supporters and servants of the state are drawn. Our army, our civil establishment, and menial attendants, are exposed to be acted on by a spark, capable of producing an explosion pregnant with danger; against which, situated as we are, it is utterly impossible to provide the slightest guard. The effect of such a shock would be the obliteration of our very name; of which not a trace would be left. Let but the present system be revised, and in time our army, and the principal servants of the state, might be furnished by a population connected by ties of consanguinity, by religion, by social intercourse, and feelings of reciprocal safety. At present we are exposed to the daily danger of utter annihilation, caused by internal rebellion, or external invasion, either of which might bring on the other. In each case we have nothing to retreat upon, or rally round; and assuredly, if once compelled to retrograde, no trace would be left behind us but the remembrance of our aggrandizement. The arguments of unjustly and forcibly displacing the present occupiers, to make room for our colonists, will, we are aware, be brought against any proposition in favor of colonization. The futility of such a puny opposition is obvious; there is not the slightest shade of similarity between our situation, and that of the Spaniards, and Portuguese, in South America. There we find the invasion of a newly dicovered country, impelled by avarice; there we find an army of strangers, roaming over a country, the inhabitants of which had, by a feeble resistance, exasperated that rage which drove them on with impetuosity in quest of wealth, as well as revenge. Horde, in succession to horde, reached that ill-fated land, in which, as the golden attraction decreased, their stay necessarily became prolonged, that they might search for that which they were aware existed. In consequence, places of abode and cultivation for their support became indispensable. The expatriation of the natives became inevitable, and their houses, women, and properties were seized. Thus the native population disappeared before rapine, murder, and oppression, while its place was occupied by the descendants of their exterminators. How essentially different would be the progress of colonization in

India. Under, a just, moderate, vigilant, and well regulated government, the interests of each class would be protected by the most rigid impartiality. The European settler, or his descendants, must come into the market like any other purchaser of land, and here our progress could not be marked, as in South America, by extirpation, and spoliation; here neither the lamentation of the widow, nor the cry of the orphan would be heard; our introduction would be attended with benefit to the people, by bringing ability, vigor, and capital into every branch of industrious labor, as it is evident, the higher classes only could colonize; agriculture would keep pace with commerce, and every species of mechanical art, emulation, moral improvement, and security would be the happy results of our amalgamation with the people of that favored but ill-fated land, whose population, so far from suffering evil at the hand of a well regulated and prudently restricted colonization, would have reason to bless the coming of a people who would lead the way to all the blessings of civilization, and to return thanks to the common Father of mankind, for conquests which, however ruinous in their immediate effects, were ultimately productive of such a glorious consummation. We must further recollect, that notwithstanding all that has been written to the contrary, India is not near populated; its finest districts, and those climates most congenial to an European constitution, are but thinly inhabited, and artizans are no where to be found out of Calcutta, and even there, very few. It by no means follows that an European capitalist, who might purchase an estate, would, as a matter of course, extirpate his native tenantry, had he the power, for the purpose of introducing an European peasantry, at an enormous expense, under the conviction that in so doing he was effectuating his irretrievable ruin. We are warned of the probable rise of the natives, should they witness the accumulation of British, or Indo-British inhabitants, lest they should ultimately subvert their religion. This is a mere scarecrow to frighten the "citizens."

The palpable contradiction which we see in the Mahomedan colonization, is a quite satisfactory demonstration of the futility of such arguments, and the absurdity of the fears to which they may have given birth. The nation, however, when the matter with which this interesting question abounds comes to be discussed, will bestow upon it that impartial and patient consideration which its importance demands.

Colonization would be pregnant with beneficial consequences to the people of India, and to the stability of our rule, inasmuch as it would create a class of subjects well-informed, and tolerably acquainted with the prejudices, manners, habits and interests of the rulers and ruled, that would eminently qualify them to fill with ability, integrity and assiduity, the subordinate situations in the revenue and judicial departments, and ameliorate the innumerable grievances the people at present suffer from abuses existing in these branches, which would necessarily give us a hold over public opinion of the greatest possible importance to the stability of our sway; as the light and energy infused into the minds of our subjects must be in proportion to the extent of our colonization; it consequently could not prove inimical to our rule until such time as the united population was capable of forming an independent power, in which British interest would necessarily be identified with the independence of British India.

The quotation from Harrington (vide Colonial Policy, page 140.) respecting the Janizaries of Turkey as bèing applicable to our situation in India, appears to be quite the reverse; the governments of the two countries are essentially dissimilar, and the constitution of the Janizaries and our Sepoys no less so; the former being literally a local military body, destitute of interest in established order, whilst the latter, being drawn from the body of the people, are absolutely identified with the continuance of our rule. The danger to which our empire is, from its very nature, exposed at present, would become gradually less as colonization increased, and we should be less liable to the immense hazard attending either external invasion or internal convulsion.

With reference to the suggestions upon this topic contained in page 223-4, of "Colonial Policy, as applicable to India," free and full participation to all qualified persons, without regard to religion, ought to be the basis of any rules relative to colonization; and natives, as well as foreigners, should be allowed to redeem the land-tax, or, in other words, become actual proprietors. Should colonization ever be admitted, and restrictions be imposed in the outset upon our native subjects, we may peradventure, instead of adding any stability to our empire, give it such a shock as will ultimately cause its fall. The effect of such restrictions would be immediate, and dangerous, if not fatal; it would be considered as an attempt to supplant the native population, by the introduction of foreigners; the tocsin would be sounded from the Himmaleah, and echoed from the Indus; discordant interests would be temporarily united by the common principle of self-preservation, and we should assuredly be considered and treated as the common enemy by every description of people throughout this mighty empire.

It is said we hold our sway in India by opinion: this no doubt may have had, and possibly still has, considerable influence in rendering it more stable; but that it is the mighty talisman by which we hold our dominion, is at once unfounded and dangerous. Our tenure may be traced to a more certain source —our army. Let that be once debauched from its obedience, that moment our rule will cease; and should Russia ever make a serious attempt upon our Indian possessions, by combining with Persia, or stimulating the Afghan population of Candhar, or the hordes of Bucharia, to join in an invasion of

India, our empire, should it escape the external assault, may, nevertheless, fall by internal rebellion. We have nothing but force to rely on; we have no population, and are considered as usurpers, by people of every degree above the cultivator and the mechanic. It cannot be concealed that their interest, pride, religion, manners, and knowledge of us and our laws, combine to generate a desire that our expulsion should be effected; and that such a sentiment would inspire a general feeling of hostility against us if the smallest hope of success was apparent, there cannot exist a doubt in any mind unwarped by prejudice, or not darkened by the decree of providence for some wise purpose beyond the scrutiny of our finite comprehension.

In conquered countries, particularly in those in which there does not exist a link between the people and their governors, dominion must be retained by a military force. Should that force belong to the nation of the conquerors, the chances of disaffection and rebellion are comparatively few, and unattended by immediate bad effects, even when they take place. But should that force have been embodied from the mass of the inhabitants of the conquered territories, as our Indian army is, separated from us by religion, manners, prejudices, and social propensities, the probability of their disaffection and rebellion will be considerably encreased, and render their loyalty and allegiance a matter of anxious and feverish solicitude, and the tenure of our dominion excessively precarious. Let our native soldiery once feel the conviction that their interests are overlooked, their prejudices unattended to, their feelings violated or disregarded, and the transition from their being the instruments of our sway to that of our downfall and expulsion, will be rapid in its progress, and in its effects fearfully awful. In such a crisis public opinion would not avail; any expectation founded upon it would prove a dreadful delusion; and those who rest secure upon such a quagmire will become, and deservedly so, the objects of contempt and derision. The magnitude of such an evil is too immense, and the occurrence of it too likely, to admit of a wise administration not applying the safest and most obvious means that human sagacity can suggest to avert such an event, or to meet it, should it come to pass, with the most powerful opposition. It is, therefore, the bounden duty of the legislature to examine strictly the system under which our Indian territories are held; and if limited colonization, progressive in its effects, hold out to its apprehension a tendency to render our rule more stable, it is incumbent on it to aid it by rescinding such parts of our present code as militate against it, and to further its progress by such new ordinances as may facilitate its commencement and completion. On the other hand, should conviction, founded on a demonstration of its baneful effects, continue to impress the mind, after a deliberate and dispassionate enquiry into all its probable consequences, the legislature is equally bound, by the most imperative and sacred duty, to oppose every attempt to carry a measure, which they may consider fraught with evil to so large a part of the human species. In adopting one of these obvious duties, the prejudices, passions and self-interest of individuals should be discarded ; for so long as these continue influential, every sentiment of the mind and every sympathy of the heart remains perverted, and it becomes impossible to survey important measures through that disinterested medium which can alone afford a correct view and a true delineation of the right course to the natural end of all legitimate government.

Our present system, to be rendered effective, must be released from the shackles with which it is bound; every obstacle to improvement must be removed; the forms and regulations which clog every department must be done away. We shall then behold that favoured region rise vigorous and triumphant from her present prostrate and inanimate condition.

It has been truly observed, " No system of government can be virtually or practically good in which the people are denied participation in the legislative, judicial, and executive branches of the state. It is obvious, that being shut out from these our unalienable rights, the prosperity of the country must suffer depression. When every department in the state is filled with foreigners, no community of opinion or feeling can exist; neither worth, nor talent can be called into action; and thus strangers, whose interests are opposed to those of the community, are left, fortified and prejudiced against the approach of truth and experience, to preside over a system degrading to the governors, and ruinous to the governed."

That such a system, in the hands of the crown, would prove strongly influential to the corruption of our constitution, and the ultimate demoralization of England, and her East Indian possessions, and reduce them to a similar condition with Spain and her South American colonies, we have the experience of the past for believing.

The fate of our predecessors, the Portuguese and Dutch, should not be disregarded; for however superior our system confessedly is to that of either of those nations, the defects which accelerated their fall are to be found in the course which we pursue, and particularly conspicuous in the jealous exclusion of our native subjects from every department of the government. The elements of the present generation are precisely what the elements of the past have been, and what the future will prove.

The fall of the Dutch sovereignty in Asia can alone be attributed to the home government having become so connected with the company, or rather, having usurped the functions which it should have watched over and controlled, but not exercised.

It may here be useful to take a brief retrospective view of the rise and fall of the Dutch in India, for the purpose of drawing the attention of the public to a subject of deep and serious importance. The unexampled rise of the Dutch to power and wealth, was owing in a great degree to the decline of the Portuguese, about the period of their rounding the Cape of Good Hope, occasioned by their being debauched by a course of success and prosperity scarcely paralleled in the history of nations. Tyrannical measures, intolerance in religious matters, and a spirit of proselytism, rendered them at once obnoxious and detestable to the people they ruled; about which time the Dutch appearing in India, the Portuguese fell without a struggle before the uncorrupted simplicity of a people destined to be their successors and rivals, who speedily became masters of all their possessions, and soon rose to the highest pinnacle of prosperity; but the constitution of this remarkably successful and powerful association was, as has been observed, defective. The entire absence of efficient controul over the governing body in Europe, and the governor-general in Asia, who held his situation for life, soon led to luxury, corruption, and vice. The greatest families in Europe possessed themselves of all the patronage, and seized the most important and lucrative situations, which descended as heir looms from one generation to another. The natural effects of such a system were, the chiefs of the nation, together with the Stadtholder, became implicated and interested in malversation. In this condition, when measures of reform became imperative, the home government, from whence they should have emanated, was, from the peculiarity of its nature, and the venality inseparable from such an anomalous system, unable and unwilling to interpose vigorous measures to rectify mismanagement, and rescue the affairs of the company from ruin.

The impunity with which misrule and cupidity indulged their views, both in Europe and Asia, served to incapacitate the constituted authorities of the republic, and the company's functionaries abroad; and to open an easy entrance to the English, who about that time appeared as actors on the great theatre of the Eastern world. England has now possessed herself of all the land and commerce of India, and has filled every civil and military situation of honour or emolument with her own sons; she has likewise subverted, in many cases, the laws and ancient customs of the people over whom she rules, and introduced her own in their stead, and these acquisitions and innovations are supported and defended by an army raised from the Indian population. In return for this, it will be asked, what has England done for India that can be considered even as a partial return for the advantages she has reaped, or the injuries she has inflicted? It may be averred, she has secured the lives and property of millions; that a man can plough his field, and reap it, that he can build a house, and live in it; and it must be acknowledged that it is so. But it is no less true, that his share of the harvest is a mere subsistence, and that his house is a mere hovel!!

If, upon the expiration of the present charter, the existing restrictions on the trade should be modified, and colonization neither encouraged, nor retarded, but left unimpeded in its natural course, and our judicial system revised, India will then become the first-born of Great Britain, and in a burst of heartfelt gratitude, and glowing eloquence, will hail her at once as a parent and friend. In the changed condition above noticed, it will remain for the legislature to determine with whom the government shall rest. This is a grave and serious question, not to be discussed and decided upon, as elsewhere observed, in the spirit or language of party or faction. Such an immense increase of patronage to the crown as would flow into the cabinet might give it an undue and unwholesome preponderance. Such a dilemma is not to be avoided under such circumstances, and as the preservation of our happy and matchless constitution must ever continue to be the dearest object of the nation, it will be cautious how it gives power to one of its parts, to the injury, if not to the annihilation of the remaining members. If this consideration be of sufficient magnitude and importance, it will possibly be conceded, that the present Indian corporation might with advantage be retained. To this it may be objected, that a community of sovereigns (for such the Court of Proprietors might be termed) would be as absurd as rare; nay, that it would be creating an opposition in the state at variance with reason, and hostile to its existence. But what would be the effect of such language? Or what would it establish? Nothing; it would be mere declamation resting upon no data; it would prove a party fiction to forward party views. In reality, such a condition would be no increase of power to the Court, which is at this moment a court of princes, the organization of which would require little, if any change. Deprive them of their worst influence, their exclusive privileges, of the principle which blights every thing it approaches—their mercantile avarice, and they will be enabled to preside with vigour over the simple and obvious duties they would have to perform.

"The East India Company is in no way advantageous as a commercial and political institution, but rather an expensive incumbrance, and an obstruction which ought long ago to have been removed." As a commercial institution, the East India Company may not have the most favourable influence upon trade, and that diffusion of knowledge and civilization which distinguishes and enlightens its track, by introducing affluence and science into every nation which opens her ports to the substantial blessings arising out of unshackled commerce. But as a political institution, it should not be rashly condemned. It has been observed in another part of this pamphlet, that the immense addition of patronage, civil and military, which the minister would derive from the possession of the entire executive government of our Indian colonies, would prove of such an overwhelming nature as to crush every parliamentary attempt to oppose his establishing an influence, injurious, if not destructive, to the principles of the constitution; and Lord Grenville's plan of selecting young men for the civil service, from our universities and public schools, and for the army, from families whose fathers have fallen in the service of the country, would be subject to serious objections, inasmuch as the youths so selected would be the children of our aristocracy, and intimately connected with parliament, and would rather facilitate than retard its corruption, by giving the guardians of our institutions an indirect participation in the corruption so much to be apprehended. The Indian service must be retained distinct and separate from the crown, and the selection of youths, if ever the Company be done away, must devolve upon some body having no connection with His Majesty's government, and the patronage in India as at present must remain in the hands of the local government; a partial change in the constitution of our present system would appear all that is requisite to the formation of an efficient establishment.

As the promulgation of the truths of Christianity, and the uncontrolled freedom of the press in India are intimately connected with the interests of our subjects, and the permanency of our sway, we shall make a few desultory remarks upon each before we leave this part of our subject, as it appears the fittest place to notice them. The importance of both these topics requires more ability than we can bring to the discussion ; we shall consequently, as in other matters deserving the most serious serious consideration, rest satisfied with bringing them under the notice of the public.

The conversion of the natives of India has apparently excited an extensive interest, and gained many adherents among the best informed classes in England, and is unquestionably a matter of deep concernment ; but in contemplating the good and evil consequences that may flow from the idea, if ever it gets abroad, that such an undertaking was meditated, we are called upon to observe the utmost caution, lest we should inadvertently afford grounds for the suspicion that government even indirectly favoured an attempt to introduce a foreign religion into the country. The most benign measures are not unfrequently followed by the most mischievous effects ; and religion, above all other concerns, is infinitely calculated to elicit the most impetuous, exasperated and sanguinary feelings. The history of the world abounds with awful lessons upon this momentous subject, interference with which, at one time or another, has proved a scourge to every nation whose annals have reached posterity. It is a powerful engine, and in unskilful hands may involve in ruin those who attempt to direct its operations. Ignorance, though audacious, is seldom so fortunate as to escape unscathed from the wrath which its presumption is sure to incur. There are but few master spirits in these times capable of allaying the storm that unwise temerity may provoke. In societies where civilization has made but a limited progress, the human mind is generally found warped by prejudice and superstition, which render it incapable of discrimination, and chain it to the popular religion of the state. To wean it from these, and awaken a deep and disinterested sense of its erroneous belief, we must enlighten it by education, and afford it the means of examining the pretensions of each persuasion previous to any attempt to influence its selection.

In acknowledging the duty of a Christian to exert himself strenuously in the promulgation of the sacred and immutable truths of the Gospel, we must not lose sight of the more paramount one conveyed by Christ himself in the following impressive words: "Whatsoever ye would that men should do to you, do ye even so to them, for this is the law and the prophets." The practice of this divine commandment is positively inculcated, the observance of it is in nowise to be evaded. How then could we reconcile it to our consciences to upbraid men who have spent their lives in the faithful performance of the rites of their religion, and their duties as fathers, friends and good citizens, with besottishly adhering to the knavish or ignorant tenets of idolatry, and denounce them as offenders against the living God, and as the rightful heirs of eternal damnation? Are we warranted in insulting the feelings and rousing the passions of men who have for accumulated ages been taught to consider their faith as an immediate emanation from divine wisdom? Or could the conduct of government be held excusable for allowing, however pure, noble and generous the motive, indiscreet zeal, or blind enthusiasm to preach under the supposed sanction of its influence, a doctrine for the comprehension of which the minds of our subjects are not duly prepared? Are we to permit fanatical bigotry to roam through the country, disseminating its doctrine in offensive language, and thereby engendering in the mind of the public the utmost alarm and solicitude for the safety of the established religion? There is nothing more likely than premature proceedings in the great work of conversion, to excite and accelerate a crisis alike fatal to our sway and the general interests of christianity. Arrogance and mistaken zeal have proved in every country of which we have any account, the greatest enemies of the Gospel. Let us, then, shun the rock upon which the best efforts of the followers of Christ to spread his religion have been wrecked, and leave the great work to the holy and pious labours of such instruments as may be ordained by heaven to perfect the object of his blessed incarnation. Let us foster the knowledge, and forward the instruction of our Indian subjects, and leave to the inscrutable wisdom of heaven the fulfilment of the word of God.

It is surprising, at a period like the present, when abundant information is every where to be found, that such erroneous conceptions regarding our Indian rule should be so generally prevalent, that we can scarcely take up a pamphlet or speech upon the most trifling subject, that we do not meet with opinions that would discredit more remote times than the era in which we live.

It appears a common error amongst the writers and orators of one party, to impute all our misrule to restrictions upon the press, and to place all our future security upon the affections of the people, which they say would follow unrestrained freedom. If an unrestricted press would carry in its train all the blessings of a free, enlightened and liberal government, who would not advocate its cause and triumph in its success? We must not deceive ourselves by such visionary expectations. The warmest advocates of a free press must admit that it is rather a part of the superstructure than the corner-stone of a great and good government; and, although quite essential to its preservation, it is not alone the fulcrum by which it can be raised into existence.

The constitution of our Indian government must undergo great changes before our possession can be looked upon as secure, or be considered mutually beneficial to England and India. To obtain this highly desirable consummation, our native subjects must be allowed to participate in the executive authority. They must have a deep interest in the stability of our sway. They must have every thing to lose, and nothing to gain, by a change, before we can securely rest on their devotion to our cause and attachment to our institutions. They must be bound to our rule by more durable links than the recorded cruelty and misconduct of their Hindoo princes "and the no less gloomy recollections of their Mahomedan masters." The memory of both is faint, and would vanish before even a remote hope of freeing themselves from the shackles of foreigners, who are looked upon as the usurpers of the government, and every respectable situation under it — as usurpers who have shackled their trade, and enslaved them to a system more inconsistent with their education, habits and prejudices, than any under which they have before suffered. With former conquerors they shared the honour and emolument of the executive authority; under our sway they share nought, but are alike shut out from every department of the state, and thrown entirely upon the precarious profits of curtailed commerce for that affluence and independence which they are precluded from sharing with their subjugators by our monopoly of every thing else.

Thus situated, how can they understand or appreciate the vituperation of an irascible and exasperated writer, or the delusive speculations of an Utopian enthusiast? No! something more tangible and substantial must be offered to their acceptance—an obvious and permanent benefit, participation in the offices under government, an efficient administration of defined and equitable law, through channels the least susceptible of fraud, corruption, and delay; all of which would spring from any salutary change in the present system, that would facilitate the access to situations of respectability and confidence of such of our native subjects, who might render themselves eligible by their knowledge of our language, literature, and laws. The establishment of colleges in the principal cities and schools at our out-stations would afford them the means of acquiring a competent education, and seminaries might be endowed with sufficient to render them objects worthy of the ambition of our European scholars, at an expense not exceeding that incurred for similar establishments in England, for a purpose which has been but partially obtained.

There cannot, it is presumed, exist a doubt in the mind of any man who has given the subject due deliberation, of the vast importance that would accrue from an order directing the business of our courts, judicial and revenue, to be transacted in English instead of Persian; such a change would at once secure the judge and client from the impositions of mercenary native expounders of law that few of them understand, and which is capable of interminable misinterpretation and evasion by those who are most deeply read and intimately acquainted with its quiddities and quirks. Then public business would no longer be impeded, nor fraud rest secure against detection, and the population would be placed in possession of the strongest possible inducement to seek an intimate knowledge of our language, manners, and institutions. Under the influence of such a change, and the strongly operating power of self-interest, and the almost certainty of realizing reasonable expectations of fortune, honour, and distinction, we should see our native subjects emerge from their present state of ignorance and degradation, and become instruments of the greatest importance in rendering our empire stable by an affectionate devotion, resting upon the best interests of those over whom we ruled.

At present, even in the absence of all inducement to acquire a knowledge of our literature and language, we see the natives forward and anxious to avail themselves of the means held out by the College established in Calcutta by the Hindoo community, with a trifling aid from the British government, to acquire all the information their instructors can communicate. Here youths, sons of the most respectable and affluent Hindoo citizens, devote themselves with assiduity to their studies, and are really in a state of forwardness, considering the very limited means within their grasp, remarkably demonstrative of the culpability of the British government for neglecting to cherish that from which the most important and beneficial results might be expected.

The aptitude of these youths, and their capacity for acquiring a distinguished proficiency in the several branches of scientific, useful and ornamental literature, from the specimens which the College, under the superintendence of Mr. Wilson, exhibit, would not suffer by a comparison with youths enjoying more extended means of instruction in Europe.

If such limited means are so productive, and hold out so much promise of an abundant harvest from a more liberal culture, how can we hope to be exonerated by posterity from having incurred the guilt attachable to a wilful neglect, from unworthy motives, of that which it was our sacred duty to perform, and which could not have failed to be beneficial and honourable to our own nation.

By educating the natives, we in a great degree secure the temporal advantage and triumph of our country, and under Providence are doing that which would prove instrumental in diffusing the divine influence of Christianity over the largest portion of the pagan world; and by neglecting to do so, we meanly resign a noble and irresistible claim to the gratitude and admiration of our Indian subjects.

If, as we are told, intellectual knowledge keeps pace with political freedom, and that science will spring up if not checked by despotic and arbitrary power, it is manifestly our bounden duty to allow as much freedom to our Indian subjects, as is consistent with the security of our sway. This proposition, it is conceived, will not be contradicted; in which case, the difficulty will be to ascertain the precise degree of restraint that will admit of the vigorous expansion of human intellect, while it checks those violent ebullitions and wild sallies, so inimical to the interests of the people, and so pregnant with danger to the existence of the state. There surely cannot exist a doubt in any well organized mind of the imperative necessity of the executive authority, in that distant country, being armed with absolute and independent power, for the application of which it can only be held responsible by the authority from whence it is derived. Turbulent, wayward, or seditious characters are by no means uncommon; so far otherwise, that they may be said to be the weeds which naturally spring up in all free communities, neither can it be denied that the judicious exercise of authority to eradicate in the germ, a plant so deleterious in its influence, would be more than was the paramount duty of those to whose hands the safety and well-being of our possessions were confided. Upon the other hand it is obvious, that the free exposure of the conduct of the executive authority would be productive of a happy and beneficial tendency, as it would necessarily render it more deliberate, rouse its energies, and stimulate it to a vigorous exertion of its faculties, that would enable it to throw off the sluggish confidence generated by the exemption of its measures from free discussion, which, like an unnatural action in the human body, taints the sources from whence nourishment is derived, and by rendering the whole mass of fluids vicious, contaminates and deranges the system. Freed from a noxious and infectious principle, a healthy action would ensue, bringing with it a communion of sentiments well calculated to excite the best sympathies of government; and, so far from weakening the tie which connects it with the vast population of the mighty empire over whose destinies it holds sway, the strongest bond of union would be produced, the obedience of the heart, the conviction of the mind—ties more durable, and affording greater stability to the state, than all the chains and trammels the invention of despotism could contrive. Hence, then, it may be allowed, that the utmost limits consistent with prudence should be granted to the press. It is sufficient that government be armed with adequate power to crush a notorious and audacious offender. Such a power, however, should be exercised under a heavy responsibility, and never put forth save when the evil was obvious and dangerous. Justice should never permit punishment to exceed crime, however mercy might be induced to temper its infliction.

JUDICIAL.

"We are the masters in India, most happily for India itself; but there are native princes in that country who would gladly recover the absolute authority that their fathers possessed. There are adventurers, and restless spirits, even in greater proportion than in Europe; who eagerly desire to see times of anarchy renewed, that their lawless and reckless ambition may once more have free scope, —the only possible means by which a hostile feeling could be excited in the great body of the people (and in that class especially who are the very sinews of our strength) against an equitable and beneficent government, the blessings of which are felt and understood."—(Quarterly Review.)

The conviction of the truth of this passage should induce us to abstain from every thing likely to rouse the dormant spirit existing in the several sources above described, and engage us to examine most carefully our institutions, for the purpose of expunging whatever we may find calculated to excite, or likely to accelerate, the crisis which must attend (however it may be susceptible of procrastination) the alarming and uncertain situation in which the British power in India exists. In the course of the present examination we shall briefly notice what is allowed to be the basis of a beneficent government—equitable, and efficient law; consequently, where the happiness of the people is the question, nothing can come in competition with it. Law is often variable, frequently unintelligible, and at variance with the genius of the people living under its influence. It therefore behoves legislators never to lose sight of the principles which should govern all law. Morality, equity, and religion, are the offspring of immutable truth, and according as we adhere to, or deviate from them, we shall be right, or in error. In forming a code for our colonies, the above fundamental principles, together with the natural disposition of the nation, should be kept constantly in view. The manners, customs, prejudices, former government, and innumerable minor considerations should be strictly attended to. The happiness of the people is the great end of all law; from it emanates the right to command, and the obligation to obey; and unless it be secured by their institutions there cannot possibly exist a legitimate pretension to command, nor an adequate motive to obedience. In reviewing our Indian system, it appears to be a fair question, whether the judicial code introduced by the British government is such, as to secure to the people, in a greater degree, the acknowledged object of jurisprudence, than their own primitive usages? If the affirmative be the case, they are beneficial; if not, the reverse is the fact.

Great and good as our government in India is, its equity and beneficence are by no means so distinctly understood, nor so thoroughly appreciated as we are led to suppose; nay, cannot be, as it is diametrically opposed to the wishes and character of the nations over which it extends. That the princes and spirits alluded to in the foregoing extract do exist, no one can pretend ignorance, who avows any knowledge of the country, the people, their institutions, civil or religious, and the system we have erected upon the ruin of their dearest interests, and fondest hopes, to the imminent risk of their utter annihilation. Let us now see how far this state of things is supported by facts. What are the interests of the people? Before we say aught upon this head, it may be necessary to observe that civil, and religious ordinances are the sources from whence every thing interesting or valuable emanates; and as mind and conscience are materially affected by education, it must follow that the moral standard of every nation upon earth will vary with their polity, ethics, and laws. Hence the reasoning applicable to one state of society, cannot be brought to bear upon another, except by way of analogy. For particular illustration we must be content to examine the people of our colonies, and their interests, by the standard of their own institutions, rather than those of which they are ignorant, or with which if at all accquainted, they know only to contemn. Let us therefore proceed to an examination of their usages, which are laws, and religion, during the earliest times of which we have any authentic history. Upon turning to their principal books of ethics we find their codes extensive, luminous, moral, and efficient; and although defaced by the accumulated distortions of fantastic fable and superstition, quite equal in all respects to the purposes of justice in civilized society, and have been considered through a series of ages from the remotest antiquity, as the ordinances of a Providence never forgetful of the necessities of mankind.

If this be the case, and the opinions entertained by the greatest legislators, that the best intended legislative provisions are of no effect unless congenial to the disposition, religion, and prejudices of the people for whom they are enacted, be true; it may be deemed unwise to interfere and substitute ordinances at variance with those rendered sacred by their origin, reverend by long usage, and respectable by their efficiency. Supposing Hindoo law compatible with a just administration of affairs, congenial to the character of the people, and all its parts in perfect unison with received opinions, what rational motive can we have for the introduction of our own or other institutions? It may be argued, as it has been asserted, that the Hindoos have no law: this is, however, a mere assertion; for as all law is acknowledged to spring from usage, we are justified in considering usage to be law. Should this not be granted, we beg to be informed what are the Institutes of Menou? or what are we to designate the contents of the "Durm Shaster," which is literally "Judicial Institutes," and in every way effective and considered by the people as the only true source of wisdom and justice? It can scarcely be necessary to remark in this place, that Hindoo law is inseparably commingled with their religious ordinances, and must necessarily be in a great measure hampered by the sophistry and superstitious ceremonies which perplex the latter, and render it capable of being used most injuriously by an unprincipled and selfish priesthood. It is nevertheless adapted to the state of society, and in conformity with the passions, prejudices, and opinions of the people, which must undergo a total change before the introduction of a new code could be met with other feelings than disgust and indignation. The sympathies and affections common to mankind in all ages and conditions, will not admit of the great body of the people viewing with indifference the subversion of institutions, cherished and revered through a long line of generations, by a code, the introduction of which not only tends to the degradation of every thing sanctified by their religion, but to loosen the bonds of society and render their religious and civil rights an object of reproach to themselves, and of contempt to other nations. Let us look to the code of our Mahomedan subjects, who are so intermixed with the Hindoos as to form but one people, as far as public opinion, feeling and language can secure a rational identity of interests. In examining the institutions introduced by them upon their conquest, we shall find they embrace a system of jurisprudence, admirably calculated, when impartially administered, to secure a fair and full portion of justice to the various classes of the people, and, under the superintendence of an English magistrate, to afford every guide the judgment can require to ensure an equitable decision, where the points litigated involve no abstract right. It would hence appear that each code is essentially efficient for the preservation of the just rights of a mixed population, whose institutions are so intimately interwoven with religious tenets, as to establish the belief of their divine origin. In such a state of things, ignorant of the manners, habits, and feelings of the great mass of the population as the wisest and best informed of our Indian statesmen and scholars confess themselves to be, it is evident the most rigid caution, the deepest deliberation, and the tenderest concern should preside over all our proceedings connected with the administration of the affairs of a people, whose destinies are subject to the control of British supremacy. In the face of the obvious policy, in opposition to our bounden duty, and in contempt of our declaration to our Indian subjects, that they should be protected in their rights according to the laws and constitution of their country, we have, instead of making ourselves acquainted with them, supplied what we considered defects by the introduction of judicial aids that are beheld with a disgust bordering on abhorrence. If the Mahomedan laws and usages, like those of the Hindoos, emanate from their religious code, which we all know to be the fact, and if the Hindoo princes of India acknowledged their rule, it would appear to follow, and not to admit of a dispute, that the laws by which India should be governed are the Hindoo laws, except where they have been superseded by the Mahomedan institutions. The fact of the Hindoos having admitted the legality of the Mahomedan sway, is rendered notorious by the circumstance of their princes having seals engraved with a legend in the Persian language, specifying, they are the servants of the reigning Mahomedan emperor; which custom, notwithstanding the Mogul is a mere pageant living upon our eleemosynary bounty, exists at the present moment. Upon the conduct of government depends the continuance and prosperity of the state, together with the lives, property, and happiness of many millions of the human species. Involving such interests, there can be no difference of opinion upon the importance of regulating our local government, so as to preserve our faith inviolate, and secure a full share of reciprocal benefit to each country. There cannot possibly, then, amongst the various subjects relative to India, be one of greater moment to the British nation, nor one more likely to excite an intense and general interest, or to call forth a greater variety of opinions, than our system of judicature in India will rouse into being, both in and out of parliament, when the period arrives for deliberating upon the renewal of the Company's charter. It has been already observed, that we are bound to preserve to our Indian subjects their rights; and that their dearest rights are their laws, for upon them depends the security of every thing rendered venerable by time, and sacred by prejudice and a superstitious respect for the observances of their forefathers. There exist in every country two descriptions of law,—usage, and written law, both of which are so blended in India with the religion of the people, that the violation of one involves interference with the other. It is evident, then, that every possible motive combines to dictate the policy of continuing to them the use of their laws when they are found to be commensurate with the ends of justice. Law, to be efficient, should be simple in its construction, be thoroughly understood, be summary in its nature, and immediate in its effects. Where law, which term we always use as synonymous to usage, is found not to answer this manifest purpose, it should be amended, provided its revision be carried into effect with extreme caution and in such places as are absolutely necessary; but never in opposition to the feelings of the people. It has been remarked by an intelligent writer, that "premature reforms should never be rashly hazarded, as they will always create doubtful feelings unless conducted with ability and consummate prudence. To reform without the necessary pre-requisites, is to revolutionize an empire: every contingent circumstance demands serious consideration: an immediate, which must be an intemperate reform, is to involve those in ruin who have not been necessary to the establishment of abuses, but derived from their ancestors a constitution with all its defects. To make such people victims of others' folly would be the height of cruelty. No reforms in any government can produce beneficial consequences, unless the welfare of the community is the primary cause of action, nor can it be reconciled to justice, equity, or even the principles of common honesty, to deprive one set of people of power and riches merely to invest these benefits in a change of men. Reform, both political and moral, is in itself very good; but reform in the body politic, as well as in the physical, must be gradual and consistent with the preservation of the whole frame. Violence does not lop off the excrescences of a tree, but roots up the tree altogether."

Trifles are, by a bigoted people, always looked upon as matters of deep importance; they should not be interfered with. When the laws we find are calculated to secure the end in view, they should be tenaciously preserved, and rigidly followed; to violate, or set them aside, and introduce others only as efficient, is wanton; tending to frustrate the object of justice, and alienate the affections of the people, whose prejudices and institutions would thus be trampled on by the very government which pledged itself to preserve and respect them. Here it may be asked, how has the sacred pledge we have given to our subjects been redeemed? Have the laws and the usages we found in the country been preserved, partially revised, or wholly set aside? Are the laws by which they have been superseded competent to the protection of the people, and the punishment of crime? And are they, in their nature and effects, summary and efficient?

We fear the most important of these questions must be answered in the negative. We have not redeemed our pledge; we have not governed them exclusively by their own laws where we could have done so. We have nothing like a competent knowledge of their laws, nor an adequate acquaintance with their social polity to permit of our performing what we have bound ourselves to accomplish. Neither are the laws we have introduced, as they are now administered, competent to the protection of the people, nor the punishment of crime; neither are they summary in their nature, nor prompt in their effect. As a proof of the adequacy of their own laws, we may refer to the reigns of Acbar and Aurungzebe for a practical proof of their efficiency, and to the common practice of their municipal polity for evidence of their fitness; and as our knowledge of them extends, we have no hesitation in declaring them capable of summary proceedings, and productive, if purely administered, of just and equitable adjudication. The propriety of these sentiments will, we trust, be evinced as we proceed.

We here beg to be clearly understood, as intending nothing beyond bringing what we consider defects in our system under the notice of the public. Our present code is a compound of Arabian, English, and Hindoo law, altogether forming a mass of indigested regulations and arbitrary proceedings, either upon the part of government or its servants, not to be paralleled in any country under heaven; proof of which will be found by the enquirer in Mill's History, and the Fifth Report of the Select Committee of the House of Commons on Indian affairs; a few instances of which we shall here submit, premising the subject with a quotation from a recent work of considerable merit, which says, "Those who have written on the affairs of India, whether as to the administration of the law, or of the revenue, have, generally speaking, got entangled in the jungles (to use an Eastern phrase), both of Hindoo and Mahomedan antiquity; some looking to Sanscrit, some to Arabic, to guide them through the labyrinth; sometimes to Hindoo law, known to be obsolete; sometimes to Hindoo history, known to be fiction; sometimes to Mahomedan law, not understood, and sometimes to Mahomedan history, not to be believed."

The above, as applied to the original institutions of the Hindoos and Mahomedans, is certainly not the case; but, to the numerous and discordant commentaries, is a correct enough picture. Let us take the common law of England, which is the unwritten law or usage, and then turn to the phalanx of expositions and annotations, and we shall not recognize, in the learned and contradictory pages of our august laws, the simple and efficient foundation upon which the present intricate and incomprehensible fabric has been raised; but on the contrary shall be forced to acknowledge, that none but those who framed the superstructure are capable of guiding us through the interminable labyrinth, alike the offspring of accumulated wisdom and sophistry.

If, then, this temple of truth requires to have, as officiating priests at the altar of justice, a body of learned and eloquent practitioners unequalled in Europe, for the purpose of distributing equity to a civilized and enlightened people, advanced to the utmost limits of every science that can expand and improve the understanding, what must be the condition of a semibarbarous people, living under its influence, without one individual, however endowed by nature or accomplished by education, in the most remote degree, capable of leading them even into the vestibule of the fane of European idolatry raised upon the ruins of their simple but efficient sanctuary? Let us proceed to the interior of the edifice, and upon the bench we shall see a judge who may have been from ten to thirty years in the country, who, having acquired a respectable knowledge of Persian (a foreign language to the natives), had been sent to the interior as an assistant to a judge, or a collector, and probably enough, from a paucity of servants, compelled to act in both capacities, in process of time promoted to a register, and called upon to decide causes to a certain amount; during the period he remains in this subordinate situation, his time is fully occupied by listening to acute litigators, and deciding, to the best of his capacity, aided by an unprincipled Moolvee, and avaricious Pundit, upon such matters as come before him. In the course of a few years he is promoted to the bench, and continues, for the remainder of his life, to preside over an extensive district, with the files of his court crowded with arrears that the longest life could not bring up. Thus situated, he daily accomplishes a meritorious drudgery, harassing to the mind and body in a degree of which none, save those who have performed it, can have an adequate idea. Thus, shut out from all intercourse with the people, except those attached to his court, the most unprincipled of their species, brought up and cherished in fraud, his mind becomes disgusted with those about him, and dissatisfied with a situation in which he daily comes in contact with crime and turpitude that evade his touch and shock his feelings; or continues to act an unsatisfactory part, exposed to the influence of wretches who may have acquired estimation in his honorable and unsuspecting mind. Whilst things are suffering perversion and distortion inside the court, to such a degree as to render detecting and unravelling them next to an impossibility, the numerous vampires outside are wallowing in the blood of those unfortunate clients, whom oppression and wrong have forced from their distant homes to seek, at the hand of British justice, a redress of grievances that may never reach the judge's ear, or if they do, continue on the files of the court during his lifetime; or peradventure these harpies of the law are employed in extorting money from ignorant and petty offenders, or innocent people, under the threat of dragging them into court on a false accusation or a frivolous pretence, and having them punished and degraded for an imputed crime. The Vakeels or attornies of these Zillah Courts are inferior to none in every thing nefarious, and unprincipled. It is a melancholy truth, defying contradiction, that our courts are generally resorted to by the rich, who can bribe the native officers to pronounce law agreeably to their wishes; the litigious, who are desirous of postponing justice or delaying the restitution of unlawful possessions; or by a vindictive and disappointed rival, who, in the words of the judge at Patna, "seeks the court as a weapon of revenge;"* those entangled in the snares spread for their destruction by the wicked contrivance of treacherous friends, or kindred at variance about the possessions of a deceased relative, which they would rather see swal-

* We are told that men of the first rank in society feel no compunction at mutually accusing each other of the most heinous offences, and supporting the prosecution with the most barefaced perjuries; nor does the detection of their falsehood create a blush.

lowed by the court, than endure the triumph of any individual of a selfish family. The police under these Zillah Courts is no less corrupt than the native law officers, who are generally a pest to society, a scourge to the district, and a disgrace to the government of which they are the unjust and unrighteous servants. During the time of Lord Cornwallis's improvements in this important branch of government were made, such as the abolition of the powers conferred on the revenue officers, the creation of Zillah judges, provincial Courts of Appeal, and the Sudder Dewanee Adawlut, with an appeal to the Governor-general in council, and finally with reference to a certain standard to the King in council; forgetful that, limiting the amount of appeals, shuts in a degree, the door of justice. It may be objected a standard is necessary to prevent frivolous unfounded appeals. But it may with justice be replied, that, under any circumstances, appeals to the last authority can never become numerous. Let us hear, however, what Mr. Mill says upon this subject.

" Among the other prejudices of those who, at this time, legislated in India with so much good intention for the people of Hindostan, were the prejudices which owe their birth to the interests, and hence to the instructions of lawyers. Of these it is one of the most remarkable, and the most mischievous, that to render judicial proceedings intricate by the multiplication of technical forms, by the rigid exaction of a great number of nice, obscure, pedantic and puzzling rites and ceremonies, tends to further the ends of justice. This unhappy instrument of justice was not forgotten in the present reforms: for courts of law provided for a people among whom justice had always been distributed in the method of simple and rational enquiry, was prescribed a course of procedure loaded with minute formalities, rendered unintelligible, tedious, and expensive by technical devices. Of the intricacy and obscurity thus intentionally created, one effect was immediately seen, —that the candidates for justice could no longer plead their own causes, that no one could undertake to present a cause to the mind of the judge according to the nicety of the prescribed and intricate forms, unless he belonged to a class of men who made it their trade to remember and observe them. A system of rules was prescribed for the formation and government of a body of native pleaders, to whom pay was provided by a small retaining fee, and a per centage on the amount of the litigated property."*

Such a system naturally involves delay and expense, and recalls strongly to our recollection the old proverb, "Where there is not cheap and prompt justice, it may be said there is no real justice," because some cannot purchase it, and the affairs of others will not admit of procrastination, more injurious to their interest than the wrong which they

* Mill's History of India, Vol. v. p. 425. 2nd col.

may be suffering. Moreover, there being no code of fixed unalterable law adapted to the necessities of mankind, by which the courts are bound to regulate their proceedings, and by which individuals could ascertain a probable termination of their suit, every thing is left to the construction which an ignorant or prejudiced Cazy or Moolvee, an equally ignorant or prejudiced Pundit, puts on an ambiguous and disputed sentence of the Koran or Shaster, or of the equally vague unwritten law of England by a gentleman who cannot have devoted his exclusive study to the attainment of a perfect knowledge of that intricate and complex science, which so frequently sets its profoundest practitioners at variance, and is too often what is caricatured by Swift, in his cause of "Bullum versus Boatum," or "Boatum versus Bullum," in his "Law is a Bottomless Pitt," or the case of "Straddling versus Stiles" of the learned Martinus Scriblerus. The opinion of one of the ablest civil servants of the Company should never cease to influence our proceedings, viz. "The nearer we approach to the rule of granting to all speedy justice without any expence whatever, the nearer we shall, in our judicial system, approach perfection." Let us see how far our present system approximates this standard. The secretary to government observes (vide Mill's 2nd edit. vol. v. p. 482.), "The Darogahs of police seldom, if ever, possess any previous instruction as to the nature and extent of their duties, nor any habits of life, calculated to enable them to perform these duties with effect. A Brahman, a Surdar,* a Moonshee, or even a menial, is each in his turn a candidate for this situation, of their fitness for which it is easy to judge; the vices which render them a pest to society, are avarice and every species of extortion." We have it again recorded in the same volume (page 501.), "It is extremely difficult, I believe I may say impossible, to arrange an effectual plan of association and co-operation among the higher orders for purposes of police, or for any other purpose. We have few large towns, no societies exercising or capable of exercising, municipal authority. There are no gentlemen in whose honour and probity, in whose spirit and activity, government can repose confidence. There exists not, between the common people and rulers, a middle order, who feel a common interest in the prosperity of the state, who love their rulers, or are by them respected." Hence it is evident the whole machine is imperfect for want of a class who do not, nor can exist under the present system. A middle class of respectable natives are thrown out of employment; none but the low and ignorant can accept of our inferior situations, and they are clothed with an authority never given to any subordinate officer in England. The whole frame of our Zillah courts would appear to demand a serious and thorough reform. The intelligent judge of Rajeshahye, as we learn from Mr. Mill, says, "In the Rajeshahye di-

* A head palankeen-boy.

vision in 1808, every day's experience and reflection on the nature our courts, and the minds and manners of the natives, serve to increase my doubts about our capacity to discover truth amongst them."

Until a middle class be established, who have an interest in the good government of the country and the preservation of the peace, a class capable, by education, and a knowledge of both European and native usage and habits, of being employed with effect, there never can be an efficient judicial or police establishment. Without such a hold, without such an aid, without such a check, what are our means of governing with advantage to the people and security to ourselves? Should any extraordinary occasion, such as external invasion or internal commotion, occur, we shall, when too late, see and feel the want of the class that could or would stand between us and the effects of a crisis which the most sanguine and enthusiastic upholder of the present condition of affairs, would be constrained to contemplate with anxiety and apprehension. Does not this melancholy condition point to the remedy calculated to supply a want so generally felt and allowed? And is not this remedy the removal of those restrictions which operate against colonization under wholesome and salutary regulations? If it is not, what then will answer the wants of government? What panacea will the timid introduce to create a middle class in society, and establish a root in the soil that will enable the British oak, planted in India, to flourish and remain unshaken during internal and external storms? It may be propped up, but props will avail not. It must be deeply fixed in the soil, or it will sicken, fade, and be laid prostrate by the first hurricane to which it may be exposed, and by its fall add another to the many lessons the world affords of the consequences of half-measures, and a timid temporizing policy, which is, at best, an unwise, ruinous and unmanly adoption of a system of expediency that has never answered any end but to expose the folly of those who resort to it. Let us now see what Sir Henry Strachey, eminent for his talents, experience and knowledge, says, as to the fitness of our present judicial system, to detect imposition or redeem truth from the well of tergiversation in which she lies immured.

"Another impediment, though of a very different nature from those I have before mentioned, and much more difficult to remove, is to me too palpable to be overlooked; I mean that arising from Europeans in our situation being necessarily ill qualified, in many points, to perform the duty required of us as judges and magistrates. Nothing is more common, even after minute and laborious examination of evidence on both sides, than for the judge to be left in utter doubt respecting the points at issue. This proceeds chiefly from our imperfect connection with the natives, and our scanty knowledge, after all our study, of their manners, customs and language. What judge can distinguish the exact truth amongst the numerous inconsistencies of the natives he examines? How often do these inconsistencies proceed from causes very different from those suspected by us? Often from simplicity, fear, or embarrassment in the witness. We cannot study the genius of the people in its own sphere of action. We know little of their domestic life, their knowledge, their conversation, their amusements, their trades and casts, or any of their natural or individual characteristics which are essential to a complete knowledge of them."

That a class upon which government could rely to furnish information relative to public feeling and popular prejudice, is a desideratum in our Indian society, cannot but strike those who even bestow the least consideration upon this momentous subject. Had a source, calculated to furnish such imperatively called for information, existed, we should not not have to record the dangerous tumults which are frequently the result of legislative acts, at variance with the character, manners and habits of Indian society. That this deficiency has continued to be felt and lamented by the ablest servants of government, has been fully shewn by the records of the state. We shall, however, furnish another opinion in addition to those already adduced, more fully to illustrate the scantiness of our knowledge, and the bad consequences resulting from our ignorance; for which purpose it will suffice to refer to a letter addressed to government in the judicial department, by the commissioners ordered to enquire into the causes of the insurrection at Barreilly in 1816; in which they remark, "In the remote provinces, particularly where the characters and dispositions, the habits and prejudices of the various and discordant classes of inhabitants cannot be intimately known to government itself; the concurrent opinion of the local functionaries, and the principal authorities, both judicial and revenue, might save government from being unguardedly led into measures which, at no great distance of time, it may be found expedient to retract. It might also be desirable that a mode could be found of learning the sentiments of well-informed natives in regard to the probable operation of any proposed law, in which (as in the present instance) government itself should have no direct interests. On such occasions the local authority might be intrusted to ascertain, from the persons of that description, how far any measures, solely intended for the protection and benefit of the natives, might be likely to militate against their feelings and prejudices." We shall now take leave of this part of our subject with a quotation from that admirable work — Sir John Malcolm's Political History of India, recently published. In describing the revolt in Rohilcund in 1816, he remarks, "The commissioners do not conceal from government their opinion that both our mode of managing the revenue and administering justice, were far from being popular with many of the principal classes in Hindostan, and they state their belief that many particular laws were highly obnoxious, as interfering with their national habits and social feelings. They further state as an admitted fact, that our courts of judicature in these provinces are viewed as grievances by the higher classes, and not considered as blessings by the lower." "To the latter," they observe, "these courts are hardly accessible from their expense, and nearly useless from their delays."

"The commissioners remark, on that indiscriminate and over-zealous activity with which the trace of public offenders has been sometimes pursued through the agency of common informers, and the summary arrests and domiciliary visits to which men of rank and respectability have been, in consequence, occasionally exposed; this they conceive to have produced an effect far beyond the immediate sphere of their occurrence."

If that class in society, the want of which is so widely felt, was encouraged, or rather not proscribed, such individuals might be every where found, and the local authorities might derive such knowledge from them as would guide the government in its legislative functions, and furnish ample proof why a law that is beneficial to one province, may prove pernicious to the interest of another. Now as difference of religion has given birth to insurmountable obstacles which effectually separate us from our Hindoo subjects, and debar us from their domestic and unrestrained society, in which we could alone find opportunities of becoming acquainted with the real feelings of the people upon matters affecting their prejudices; it behoves us not to discourage the growth of that class which, by approximating to an equality with the great body of the people, would naturally, in the common intercourse of society, become acquainted with every essential. Again, it would be accordant to the principles of justice and humanity, as well as infinitely advantageous to the local government, to allow the higher classes of our subjects some participation in the advantages derivable from the many honourable and lucrative employments in its disposal, which might be accomplished with advantage to our judicial, revenue, and police departments, without incurring additional expence. To effect this, a partial change in these departments would apparently answer the end in view; but as prejudice in favour of established rules requires not only the fullest conviction of their inadequacy, but the most distinterested manner of thinking, there will necessarily be many difficulties opposed to the introduction of improvements that, at first sight, may have the appearance of militating against the interest of the European establishment of our Indian government. Nothing, consequently, but the ardent desire of improvement, with a frigid regardlessness of the murmurs of interested people, can effect that reorganization of our executive system, which is indispensably necessary for the perfect administration of justice, and the greater security of our sway over our vast dominions. It may be objected, that allowing the respectable part of the native population a participation in the administration of affairs, would be laying the foundation of a system calculated to weaken, rather than strengthen, the hold we have at present over the obedience of our native subjects. This, if likely to be the result, would be a sufficient cause for abstaining from the slightest innovation on the present order of things. Unfounded fears have ever been a bar to improvement; all objections, therefore, should be scrupulously examined before they are allowed to operate against the introduction and trial of an apparently wise and beneficial policy. Under the impression, however erroneous it may be, that there is both wisdom and advantage to be expected from a change, we shall succinctly touch, in another place, upon the outlines of measures apparently calculated to correct many of the existing abuses, and greatly aid the judicial servants in the performance of their Augean labour. Melancholy as the foregoing detailed condition of our judicial system in India is, it is not all; for unequal as such an incongruous and ill-adapted code is to the distribution of prompt and effective justice, it is rendered still more defective by the want of servants who can be relied upon to preside over our tribunals. That this deficiency cannot be supplied, we have the best possible assurance, that of the Select Committee of the House of Commons, viz.

"When any great public duty is to be performed, and the number of performers is found to be too small for the demand, the most obvious of all expedients is to encrease the number." With regard to this expedient for enabling the government in India to do justice between its subjects, the Committee of the House of Commons made an extraordinary declaration in 1802, "An augmentation in the number of European judges adequate to the purpose required, would be attended with an augmentation of charge, which the state of the finances is not calculated to bear, and the same objection occurs to the appointment of assistant judges." What, then, is to be done? Are the just claims of seventy millions to be set aside, lawless aggression of every description sanctioned, inadequately punished, or not entirely suppressed, because the finances of the state are said to be unequal to the payment of a competent preventive police, and an efficient judicial establishment? Such a question is assuredly not to be asked in an age mature in every liberal science. It is obvious, that if the easier attainment of justice be essential, the judicial branch of the service should be increased, let the expense be what it may. It ought to be placed in a condition commensurate to the demands of the country, unless some equally efficacious but less expensive remedy can be contrived to meet the necessities of the state. In such a dilemma one would think the establishment of the Punchait system, which has under all the native governments in India been found most beneficial, might be resorted to with advantage without the slightest detriment to the sacred ends of justice, more especially as the British government is pledged to observe inviolate the rights of the natives. This system, salutary and simple as it is, has its opposers, but it has also enlightened advocates, whose experience has afforded them an opportunity of forming a dispassionate estimation of its merits. The arguments of the former do not appear tenable; the system appears nearly if not exactly, to resemble in the simplicity and purity of its construction, our English jury; the gigantic defender of the rights of the people against the sophistries of law, the corruption of wealth, and the influence of power. Why then, since it is congenial to the disposition, adequate to the necessity, familiar to, and revered by every class of society, and unattended with expense, trouble, or delay, should it be withheld from those by whom it is unanimously approved, and whose rights we have bound ourselves to preserve? It will not suffice to say it has failed in this or that instance, in this or that country; we must prove its notorious inutility, and failure in India. Unless the decriers of this adequate medium of meeting the wants of the public can do so, they can do nothing. Declamation, however specious and eloquent,—argument, however subtile and ingenious, must yield to the test of experience; and in this instance, the very organization of a court of

Punchait, offers a full refutation to every objection that has hitherto been brought against it. Previous however to noticing it, we solicit the reader's attention to the opinion of the Select Committee, on the delay of bringing criminals to trial, and the hope expressed that some plan might be introduced to mitigate its effects; with respect to which, the committee observes, "It is probably not so great as when formerly it was the subject of objection to the then existing system; it still appears to occur in a degree productive of evil, and which it should be the object of government to remove." In continuation of this subject, the committee further remark, "Expedients have been resorted to for the purpose of relieving the judge, by enlarging the limits of causes referable from him to his register, and to the native commissioners, by limiting the term for appeal. Something however is yet wanting to complete that system of speedy justice, both civil and criminal, which Lord Cornwallis was so desirous of introducing, but which has not yet attained that degree of excellence of which it may be still hoped it is susceptible." We now beg the reader's attention to the following slight outline of the prominent features of a court of Punchait. The complainant and defendant, each choose one, two, or three, individuals to whom the Potail of the village, or the Cazy of the town, adds a foreman, or Mookh, or the litigants themselves fix upon some person to preside over the Punchait, which is generally composed of the class to which they belong. Its business is to examine witnesses, institute investigations, and is at once deliberative, inquisitorial, and arbitrative. In every village or town, there is generally of each class or trade, one whose eminent and acknowledged integrity has secured him the distinguished preference of being selected to preside as Mookh, over all Punchaits composed of the tribe to which he may belong. The love of fame, and that virtuous ambition which is generally diffused throughout the human species, whether in a civilized, or savage state, is a most effectual guard against a partial or a flagrant departure from equity, by a court thus constituted. The moral consequences attending an individual who has swerved from a conscientious discharge of his duty, as an honest man, and good citizen, are so immense, that nothing could compensate for it. The slightest deviation would become a matter of notoriety; the forfeiture of character would follow, which, to a tradesman, a merchant, or a banker, would inevitably lead to ruin. The writer has presided over three large districts, in which the inhabitants were mixed, and in a great measure degraded, and had no other assistance than that afforded by the usage of the country, and the people; and in justice to both, is bound to bear testimony to their perfect adequacy to the legitimate ends of a good government. Inefficient as they may be supposed, it is satisfactorily established that their very nature, renders them infinitely superior to our own courts in all petty and litigious disputes between natives. We are told in the Fifth Report of the Select Committee, that more causes remained on the files of the Zillah Courts of Tirhoot, Dacca, Jellalpore, and Bahar, than had been dismissed from them in five years. This condition of our judicial system would seem to warrant the query which the Court of Directors seriously apprehended, and feelingly express in their Revenue Dispatch to Fort St. George, 26th March 1812: "We should be very sorry that from the accumulation of such arrears there should ever be room to raise a question whether it would be better to leave the natives to their own arbitrary and precipitate tribunals, than to harass their feelings, and injure their property, by an endless procrastination of their suits, under the pretence of more deliberate justice."—Daily experience and the concurring opinion of our best servants answers this query in the affirmative. Let the liberal and enlightened judge of Bahar speak upon the occasion: "The commitments for the breaches of the peace arising from boundary disputes, and other contests concerning landed property, are ascribed to the great, though unavoidable arrear of untried causes pending in some of the courts; since by necessarily protracting for years the decision of suits, it frequently drove the suitors to despair, and induced them to run the risk of taking justice into their own hands, by seizing the object in dispute, rather than await the tardy issue of a process which threatened to exceed the probable duration of their own lives." Having in the course of this chapter, fully, and, we hope, satisfactorily displayed the inadequacy of our judicial establishment, we shall now advert to the amendment we would, with due and deferential consideration, recommend to the notice of those presiding over our Indian possessions. Instead of petty disputes from distant villages being brought for decision to our Zillah Kutcherries, the Potails, or heads of the villages, should be authorized to take cognizance of them to a certain extent, reporting the proceedings of the Punchait to an authority established for the purpose. No cause should be received by the superior authorities that had not first been preferred to the Potail, and from him, regularly up through each intervening tribunal. By this means, the time of the industrious would be saved, and the knavery of the litigious would be frustrated; our courts would cease to be overloaded with business; the contamination that pervades their proceedings would in a great measure, be curtailed; and its baneful effects confined to its immediate vicinity. Momlutdars in the several Purgunnahs, avowedly men of property, and respectability, and selected from the first families in the district, with due attention to talents and character, should be nominated, with an adequate salary, and should, in addition to their fiscal duties, be empowered to assemble Punchaits to take cognizance of all disputes commencing where the Potail's authority ceased, and extending to another fixed sum and crime: appeals lying from the Potail's decree to the Punchaits assembled under the sanction of the Momlutdar, who should report in writing to the Judge's, or Collector's Kutcherry. Here there might be two other officers, one in a judicial, the other in a fiscal capacity, and designated Native Assistants to the judge or collector. Their business should be to receive appeals from the Momlutdar's courts, investigate the matter, and send it up to their superiors. These should be the highest grade, and be nominated by government, and allowed a handsome salary. At this point should commence our European establishment—an assistant judge, and an assistant collector, whose duty it should be to receive and submit all extraordinary cases to their chief, with such matter as might be elicited in the course of their investigation. Such an arrangement could not but be attended by beneficial effects, both to government and the community; its immediate advantage would be the acceleration of justice in every department, and doing away the complaint so common throughout our provinces, of the impossibility of getting through the heavy duties imposed upon our civil servants, and the consequent clogging of the wheels of justice; and in many cases its utter extinction. It would likewise tend to create an upper order in our native society, which would not only improve their moral character, through the medium of example, but serve to bring us more immediately into contact with them, than the present system, by which, both parties would be benefited by a reciprocal knowledge of each other. We should hence gain a stronger hold upon their affections through the all-powerful motive of self, and their interest in the existence of an establishment in which they had solid advantages at stake.

As a code of good laws, founded upon wisdom, is held to be the noblest present that can be made to a nation; so is an ambiguous code the greatest evil under whose withering influence a people can languish. Let us then conscientiously endeavour to deserve the acclamation of the present generation, and the gratitude of posterity, by revising and correcting our Indian jurisprudence, keeping steadily in view, during the progress of our reformation, that man has in all ages of the world been a slave to habit, and averse to innovation; that the operation of any change is always difficult, and frequently hazardous; that the public mind once convulsed, is not easily tranquillized. Consideration for the superstitions of our subjects, and delicacy in the treatment necessary for their removal; dexterity in seizing the time for introducing changes with precaution, and address in effecting them, will go far to crown our efforts with success. By such a course, England will challenge the admiration and applause of Europe, whilst she secures the affection and devotion of her Asiatic subjects.

Perfection, we are told, is not to be obtained in jurisprudence; we must be satisfied with a predominant good, and leave our subjects to the enjoyment of their ancient establishments, until their mental acquirements, which we are bound to aid and further, fit them for other constitutions, until which period, we should respect their usages, wherever we find them better calculated to secure the obvious ends of justice, than the more elaborate and more expensive system introduced by a benevolent but mistaken notion.

TERRITORIAL.

In conquered countries in Asia the natives cannot set up a claim of inherent right arising out of previous possession, for the very act of conquest subverts all former rights, and transfers the conquered country to its new masters. Policy and expediency however will, no doubt, induce conquerors to respect all public possessions and, as far as is consistent, the properties of their new subjects. This has been the case in India. The Mahomedan emperors seldom interfered with the usages of the people, nor disturbed by sudden and violent innovations the simple, yet efficient institutions long established throughout India, from which the proprietary rights of the cultivator have been set up, instead of his real rights, those of occupancy. This question has been and continues a fruitful source of discussion and disagreement to all who have written upon landed tenure in India. To enter upon a subject that has divided the opinions of our best informed and dispassionate Indian historians and statesman, would be at once useless and presumptuous; as it is not likely that those who have professed to have taken pains and trouble to obtain data for the opinions they advocate, would be disposed to relinquish them, without that sort of proof which our meagre and equivocal historical information does not pretend to afford. We shall therefore leave the several parties in the undisturbed possession of the opinions which they have so stoutly maintained. As far as information upon this knotty point is required for all practical purposes, it will suffice for our object to take Mahomedan law for our guide in all discussions subsequent to the Mogul conquest; and the immemorial usage of the Hindoos as handled down through each successive generation in matters anterior to that date. With reference to the first, we learn that all conquered countries belong to the Mussulmans, and that the leader of the conquering army, or the king, is merely the guardian of the rights of the community, and that Jagheers are nothing more than an appropriation of the revenue of the land, and that even an alienation of the revenue by the crown is restricted; and although such grants are inheritable, it by no means follows they are transferable. We are further informed by Mahomedan history, that upon the occupation of a newly acquired country, the people were frequently left to the undisturbed possession of the lands, upon stipulating for the payment of a tribute; and that their embracing the faith led to better terms being granted. From this it would appear, the land was held in trust by the sovereign, on the part of the commonwealth; the proprietary right therefore is virtually, for all practical purposes, lodged in the state. In those parts of India into which the Mahomedan influence found its way without deposing the native princes, we find the system of village communities (for a description of which see "Central India," vol. ii.) universally prevalent, and all revenue settlements concluded upon the part of government with the Potail, aided by the Putwarree and some of the oldest and most respectable inhabitants. The limits of each village are ascertainable by established marks, and the land is not alienable. The right of occupancy by the cultivator being as indefeasible as that of proprietor by the state, Zumeendars or Jagheerdars cannot have a claim for aught beyond the terms of their assignments: the former were generally collectors or farmers of revenue; the latter servants or pensioners of the state. Under native governments there is no individual right acknowledged that has not been derived from the state; and all Zumeendaree claims about which so much has been written, were rather honorary and nominal than real; as they are seldom found to consist of more than a few trifling fees of office of different denominations, indicative of former rights long since usurped or set aside. The claim, therefore, of Zumeendaree rights has no tendency whatever to hamper our revenue proceedings, and, however interesting it may be as an historical speculation, should be disregarded as a claim to the proprietorship of land. The fees of Zumeendars are their only pretensions; they should be respected, and with them they are generally content. Should any reform in the revenue branch of our Indian government be contemplated hereafter, it will remain with the home authorities to decide between the systems of Lord Cornwallis and Sir T. Munro, either of which must be generally adopted. There is no alternative; we must either admit the purchase of substantial proprietary right, or follow the Ryotwaree system. The former of these has been fairly tried on a large and liberal scale, and has completely failed; instead of proving what it was intended it should be—a blessing to the country, it turned out a curse; previous to the illustration of which, we shall give a short sketch of its origin and progress, and then quote the sentiments of our revenue officers in their own words. Upon Lord Cornwallis's appointment to the governor-generalship of India, it was averred by the then authorities, that our financial system was bad. That the frequent substitution of farmers, and temporary agents, for the permanent Zumeendars, the failure of all attempts to increase the revenue, and the exclusion of collectors from a share in forming the assessments, were all liable to censure. Complaint was made of the heavy outstanding arrears of the last four years' settlement, and of the exhausted, and impoverished state of the country. To improve this condition of things, it was ordered, that the settlement should be made with the Zumeendars, for a period of ten years, and to be ultimately permanent. That collectors of revenue should be invested with judicatory, and magisterial powers. This settlement with the Zumeendars, who were in fact nothing more than revenue collectors, upset at once the rights of the inhabitants, and the immemorial usages of the country; the Zumeendars never having possessed even the shadow of a proprietary right, which belonged exclusively to the crown, and that of occupancy to the Ryots, and village communities. The proceeding was consequently unjust, and an ignorance disgraceful to the government, which, in lieu of the robbery committed, decreed, that the Zumeendar or collector should give the Ryot a permanent lease of his lands, at such a rate as the Zumeendar's discretion might dictate, instead of enforcing long leases, or making their tenure as perpetual and unalterable as that of the Zumeendar. In default of payment of their taxes by the Zumeendars, Government reserved to itself the power of selling such portion of land as might be equivalent to their arrears; the effect of which was the virtual abrogation of the permanent system, and the introduction of a confusion, uncertainty, and beggary, to which the country had happily been a stranger in the most desolating period of Mahomedan ignorance and despotism. Upon this subject we are informed by that enlightened and profound historian, Mr. Mill, that "Government had established courts of law, and appointed for them a numerous list of forms, through which it required much time to pass. In their own case, however, it would, they perceived, be highly desirable to obtain speedy justice. To obtain speedy justice they saw it would be absolutely necessary to be exempt from technical forms. To what expedient then had they recourse? To the abolition of technical forms? No indeed! They made a particular exemption of their own case. They enacted, that in all suits for rent or revenue, the court should proceed by summary measures; nay, further, that in such suits the proceedings should be exempted from those fees and expences to which other candidates for justice were appointed to submit. By a high and conspicuous act, more expressive than words, they declared that one thing was conducive, or rather essential to justice; and established, by their legislative authority, the very reverse." We shall now proceed to the opinions before alluded to.

Our revenue system, according to the arrangements introduced by Lord Cornwallis, is thus described by the collector of Midnapore in a letter dated 1812. "All the Zumeendars with whom I have ever had any communication in this and other districts, have but one sentiment respecting the rules at present in force for the collecting of the public revenue. They all say that such a harsh and oppressive system was never before resorted to in any country; that the custom of imprisoning landholders for arrears of revenue was, in comparison, mild and benevolent to them; that it was no doubt the intention of government to confer an important benefit on them; by abolishing this custom, it has been found by melancholy experience, that a system of sales and attachments has in a few years reduced most of the great Zumeendars in Bengal to distress and beggary, and produced a greater change in landed property, than has ever happened in the same space of time in any age or country, by the mere effect of internal regulations?

The collector of Burdwan, in a letter to the Board of Revenue says, "The Rajah of Burdwan begs leave to submit to your consideration whether or not it can be possible for him to discharge his engagements with the British government, with that punctuality which the Regulations require, unless he be armed with powers as prompt to enforce payment from his renters, as government had been pleased to authorize the use of, in regard to its own claims; and he seems to think it must have proceeded from an oversight, rather than from any just and avowed principle, that there should have been adopted two modes of juridical process, under the same government; the one summary, and efficient in the satisfaction of its own claims: the other tardy and uncertain, in regard to the satisfaction of the claims of its own subjects; more especially, in a case like the present, where ability to discharge the one demand, necessarily depends on the other demand being realized."

Such a monstrous anomaly in our reformed revenue regulations as that complained of, has not a parallel in any code with which we are acquainted. In fact the system altogether appears to be a wanton infraction of the rights of the community, an un warrantable and forcible robbery of the people for the purpose of establishing upon a rotten foundation an order in society, that had never existed, the constitution of which was incompatible with the existence of and at variance with the sacred and ancient institutions of the country. The pernicious and ruinous consequence of such censurable precipitation, has been widely and severely felt, occasioning in its extensive course animosities and calamities, from which the simple code of their fathers had, up to that fatal period, exempted them. We learn from the history of this much-to-be-reprobated and deplorable innovation, that the beneficent object intended by the projectors of the scheme entirely failed; that instead of creating the intended aristocracy, it but served to enlarge the bounds of desolation, drawing into its irresistible vortex the whole mass of the landed society, confounding and overwhelming all in one common and irretrievable ruin. It is stated that the amount of land advertised for sale in one year exceeded 28,70,000, rupees, and that the process of a civil suit in one of the Zillah Courts for the recovery of arrears of rent, would occupy a longer time than the " ordinary period of human life." Enough has surely been learnt from experience, to induce the most sturdy admirers of the permanent system to yield to the generally prevailing opinion of its inutility. It is time that the public mind should be made up as to the system best calculated to secure to government, without injuring the cultivator, the greatest advantage that can be derived from the land, consistent with the comfort and happiness of the people; and it may be conceded that the village system, deprived of its frequent vexations, and over-assessments, is the one most consonant with the interest of the state, the comfort, security, and happiness of the cultivator. A few years' experience would, we imagine, serve to afford ample data for an equitable assessment, which should be subject to revision at intervals of five, ten, fifteen, twenty, twenty-five, thirty, forty, fifty, even to one hundred years; but never beyond that period; at the expiration of which a fair maximum, equal to contingencies on both sides might be fixed upon for a still longer period of lease. By the adoption of some such measure the rights and comforts of society would be secured, the government be protected from a fluctuating revenue, and our Zillah Courts freed from the greatest part of their troublesome and difficult duty. In forming such arrangements, government would of course adjust its leases, so as to leave the tenants merely sufficient to furnish stock, and defray labour, together with the ordinary profits of farming. If, therefore, the greatest possible advantage that can be derived from lands consistent with the well-being of the tenant, be the object of those states whose income is derived from the land, it is evidently beneficial to make agreements with the cultivator, or to have as few mediums between the lord paramount and cultivator as the nature of the transaction will admit; for each mediator must have a profit to enable him to live, and each superior grade will naturally exact as much from its inferior as it can, until it comes down to the cultivator, who is left to languish in poverty, with a bare subsistence. That this must necessarily be the result of all Zumeendaree systems, is now indisputably known. An examination of Lord Cornwallis's settlement 1793 will prove the fact: by far the greater part of those who were vested with lands to which they had not the shadow of a right, have been obliged to sell, wholly or in part, their estates, to make good the defalcation of rents. In consequence of which, land, instead of remaining, as it had continued for ages, and as we found it, the property of the state, paying fees in lieu of labour to those who had charge of and cultivated it, was unjustly and forcibly made the personal property of an individual who was never any thing in the estimation of our Mahomedan precursors, but a collector. The almost universal exclamations which have been uttered against the Zumeendaree system would appear sufficient to warrant a deviation from it, where we have made no promise to the people, and where it does exist, it would prove advantageous to purchase the rights and allow the revenue branch of our system to resume its former character, as any deviation from it is considered by the country to flow rather from ignorance than liberality. So long as our settlements are made through the medium of our European collectors, directly with the heads of villages, founded upon an exact knowledge of the arable, cultivated, and waste lands, will our assessments be susceptible of increase, till we arrive at the maximum rent the land can defray, which will not be till all the waste lands fit for cultivation be redeemed; and as the population is infinitely below what the land can provide for, our revenue will not have arrived at its maximum for ages to come. In the Zumeendaree system, it is the object of the Zumeendar to receive the greatest rent he can derive with the least trouble; and as there will always exist needy adventurers, ready to sacrifice the well being of others to their own ends, there will necessarily exist a competition for the farms; and to secure the full benefit to be derived from such an unnatural state of things, short leases must be resorted to, and thus, every intermediate degree from the Zumeendar to the cultivator, is exposed to an extortion, and oppression, which ends only in poverty and ruin. The greater exertions the tenant makes to improve his lands, the more keen in proportion becomes the insatiable avarice of the superior; the effect of which is displayed by the penury and misery of the actual cultivators. It hence follows, that as the lower classes are deprived of increased means, the increase of population is impossible. Let this vitiated policy be changed, and increased means will be attended by an increased population; the consequence of which will be the redemption of waste lands, and an increased revenue to the government.

The dense population of Bengal may be set forth as a proof in contradiction of what has been stated; but it must be recollected, that Bengal is in a great measure independent of agricultural profits, and that it is full of British subjects, independent of the great landholders whose tenants they are, and whom they cannot oppress; and that the lower orders are generally labourers and mechanics, less connected with the soil than any other people in India.

There cannot, in reason, be any objection brought forward against such a course, as there is not a state in India, even among the Rajepoots, whose usages have been least affected by the Mahomedan conquest, where the sovereign has not assumed proprietary rights. The Bheels, Meenahs, and Goojers were the possessors of Central India previous to its conquest by the Rajepoots, and where are we to look for their unviolated rights as sovereigns? If abstract opinions of right are to govern our proceedings, let us restore the dominions we have subjugated to the Takoor of Beadlah, in Meywar, the lineal descendant of the renowned Pirthee Raje; and the sceptre of the great Mogul to the feeble grasp of his degenerate and nominal successor, and rest content with a free trade to the several ports in India. Or, let us cease to view this question in any other light than as an amusing speculation, or historical research. Why investigate a question for the guidance of our conduct, that opposes no obstacle to our interests? Is it not sufficient to respect the usage we find in force? Why should we seek to act upon systems long since forsaken, or upon laws that have been obsolete or nugatory for ages? In considering the merits of each system separately, it would appear that the over-assessment of the Ryotwaree, with the vexatious interference consequent upon an annual arrangement, and the under-assessment of the permanent system, with the insurmountable difficulties the Zumeendars experience in realizing their rents, together with the gross oppression of the under Ryots by the middlemen, are evils which require a remedy. Hence it follows, that what we should attend to, is the interests of government, and the rights of the people, with a view to which we should so regulate our revenue measures, as to preserve both, and secure each a full enjoyment of its legitimate rights, leaning somewhat to the side of the latter. A substantial population is evidently the strength of the government; its opulence and well being is the source from which our exchequer is replenished. A middle course is obviously the one we should pursue.

> "Princes and lords may flourish, or may fade,
> A breath can make them, as a breath hath made,
> But a bold peasantry, a country's pride,
> When once destroyed can never be supplied."

Next in magnitude, and importance to our land-revenue measures, come our salt and opium monopolies, the produce of which forms a considerable item of our receipts; they consequently merit sober deliberation. It is generally understood, and we believe justly so, that the manner in which our salt is procured, is productive of infinite misery to those employed in its manufacture. Mr. Tucker, in his review of the financial state of the East India Company, expresses his sentiments on our salt monopoly in language which bespeaks the statesman and philanthropist, and they will unquestionably attract the attention of parliament when the time comes for revising our present system.

Agreeably to this gentleman's statement, our profits upon this monopoly average an immense sum, which consideration induces him to advocate the tax, although he admits to a certain extent the objections to which it is obnoxious.

Salt, however, being an indispensable article, and one that must be procured at any hazard, by all classes, should, we think, be left unshackled to the public. Why not leave the greedy cupidity of the capitalist to bring it into the market, and by a fair competition, allow the lower orders a free and unrestrained use of this simple necessary of life. Would not a prohibition to sell the article without a licence suffice, and would not a tax upon such a licence answer our object?

Our opium monopoly is another lucrative branch

of revenue, and although not attended with the loss of life, and actual misery consequent on the other, is, notwithstanding, an oppressive evil to the inhabitants of our own provinces, and a source of certain destruction to the inhabitants of the territories of our allies, as well as a most vexatious interference with their legitimate rights, although guaranteed by ratified treaties. Central India is exclusively an agricultural country, depending entirely on the productions of the soil. The staple commodity is opium. Sugar, cotton, and grain are bulky articles, the exportation of which is attended with an expense which renders them but little, if at all, productive articles for external commerce, as they are undersold by other districts nearer the sea, which have the advantage of water-carriage. Grain too, which in times of commotion was cultivated in small quantities, has, with the other blessings attending peace and security, become a drug; every district yielding tenfold the quantity required for consumption. In this dilemma, opium presented a certain source of profit to the states, and a comfortable independence to their subjects, till our necessities, aided by the irresistible influence of power, seized upon the only source from which they could with any certainty look to derive a profitable return. Monopolies in their very nature are bad; they are the resort of an unwise policy, and a thirst for gain. They are well described as being "the device of improvidence, which, for a present advantage, wastes the resources of futurity."

We are told that the measures here reprobated, are indispensably necessary for the Company to provide for the payment of a dividend at the rate of ten per cent. Against the validity of such an argument we must protest. Why should one body be pampered with an interest branded by parliament as illicit, and inadmissible to the rest of the nation?

It is certain there has never been a case made out by the Court of Directors that would justify a dividend of ten per cent.; because the reason assigned—the credit of the Company failing, and the stockholders selling out, and the Company thereby becoming insolvent,—is ridiculous, a mere bugbear to silence the ignorant and alarm the timid. Dividing ten per cent. will not supply funds to meet bills payable within a certain time; it will rather deprive them of ultimate means, by taking away their present resources. The idea of foreigners becoming alarmed at there being no dividend, is so flimsy as not to merit a moment's thought. The debates in the House of Commons on the subject, proclaimed the true state of the Company's affairs, and afforded the nation at large, the best ground upon which an opinion approximating to truth can be formed; added to which, preventing a dividend would be attended with more salutary and immediate consequences to the finances, than a dividend of fifty per cent.; the one would serve to nurse and cherish the means, the other but serves, by lavish expenditure, to increase embarrassment; ruinous in its consequences to the corporation and the state. The idea that foreign proprietors would take alarm and sell out, is at once puerile and preposterous. The very circumstance includes a purchaser as well as a seller, and where lies the difference to the corporation who holds the share? Scandinavian, Turk, Jew, or Hindoo, it is the same to the state. The sale of shares by foreigners would obviously prove beneficial, inasmuch as the dividend, when shared, would be received and spent in England. Moreover, the dividend appears incompatible with a fair, efficient, and good government; contrary to the first principles of all associations, and substantial and reciprocal benefit. The principle of the dividend would seem to be as unsound, as its practice is pernicious. What advantage does a proprietor of Indian stock derive exclusive of his dividend? None; those about London may, and do, no doubt, derive great advantage by making their votes upon particular occasions serve as a provision for their offspring or connections; but the majority of stock is held by foreigners, or individuals away from London, whose inducement is the mere dividend, and nothing else. Hence it would appear that the sure passage into the Direction was through the favour of the proprietors; consequently the most obvious road to their favor is their interests, that is to say, keeping up or increasing the dividends. Let us see how this is accomplished, either by borrowing at a ruinous interest, or by forcing capital to provide investments from India, which yield little return, the principal portion of the product being wasted through the countless and endless ducts in which it flows from Leadenhall Street into every kingdom in Europe. Thus this unjust and vicious distribution is fraught with the most perilous consequences: it may justly be considered a nightmare which lies heavy on the bosom of our Indian possessions; and renders its breathing and the circulation languid unto death, requiring, at times, a gigantic struggle to shake off the torpor which threatens its existence.

COMMERCIAL.

As security for property, and unrestrained freedom of industry, are admitted to be essentially necessary to commerce, it follows that, as the system of our commercial intercourse with India assimilates, or differs from the above admission, it must be acknowledged good, or pronounced defective. To determine which of these results is the fact with respect to our Indian trade, it will be expedient to examine the principles by which it is regulated, and their effects. As we are not sufficiently versed in political economy to guide us through the labyrinth of exchange, labour, and all the arcana of this complex question, we shall avoid the discussion of a subject which can alone be set at rest by public opinion, and remain satisfied with drawing the observation of those interested in the question to a topic, above all others indissolubly interwoven with the general weal. We shall therefore, in this place, merely advert to the most obvious principles of this intricate, and important matter. We are informed by those acquainted with that science, that so long as the revenues of a state only, are applied to the production, it is evident it can never exceed a certain amount; but that when the resources of another state are brought into action, the product must increase in a proportion equal to the increased means. Again; if the industry of a nation is equal to its capital, the deterioration of the former will diminish the latter. It therefore follows, so long as capital increases, industry cannot deteriorate. We are further told that commercial countries derive benefit only from their imports, and that exclusive bodies, although supported by privileges and monopolies, are the worst media through which a nation can carry on its foreign commerce. It must never be forgotten that when such bodies come to lose in part, or wholly, their commercial character, and assume that of sovereign, they not only become a still more unfit medium, but obtain a power inimical to the best interests of the state to which they belong, and ruinous to that over which they preside. For it is not to be expected they will abstain from using their executive influence, in a manner subservient to their commercial objects. The love of gain is not only the motive for trade, but the life and soul of commercial enterprize, and where authority can be brought to aid it, we must not depend upon the precarious virtue of a trading corporation, that no injuries are committed, nor unjustifiable measures adopted, to secure the greatest advantage derivable from a possession held under an uncertain tenure. Indeed, the history of all such bodies is fraught with matter amply sufficient to prevent us from dwelling with any thing like hope upon the expectation of finding a noble disinterestedness in the character of exclusive corporations. Hence it follows as a matter of course; that a free trade would prove beneficial to both England and India. Is not then the supineness of the British nation relative to Indian affairs, a surprising and melancholy instance of the entire absence of foresight, where we would be induced to look for the keenest discernment, roused into active being, for the purpose of applying a remedy for the starving condition of our manufacturing population, the encreasing embarrassment of our domestic commerce, and the generally prevailing distress obvious throughout the land? Indian commerce, if placed upon an equality with that of our other possessions, would prove valuable to England in a greater degree than all her colonies. Vast as is the importance of the subject, it appears to be treated with an indifference apparently the result of a questionable policy, at variance with the true interests of the British empire.

If the paralyzing duties laid upon the produce of the East Indies be necessary for the welfare of the merchants concerned in the West Indian trade, and the interests of those collaterally connected with it, it would appear to be a fair question, whether it would be more beneficial to the country at large to appropriate the million and a half which our colonies cost the nation, to those who would suffer by throwing open our East India trade, and reducing the duties to a level with those of our other colonies, or allow it to remain as at present?

As the time is fast approaching, when this consideration will force itself upon the public attention, we earnestly hope the community at large will be prepared to argue upon the broad principles of common equity, a matter with which the best interests and dearest rights of the nation are inextricably blended.

We are told, by a recent writer of considerable experience and talent, that "It yet remains a problem, whether the possession of India should be considered as a source of treasure or weakness to the mother country." We must, therefore, understand, (and yet it appears incomprehensible,) that the immense importation and considerable exportation by which a great demand for labour is occasioned, is of no advantage, but a mere speculative question — an ideal good — a theory not to be solved by the experience of more than half a century. It is high time that the legislature should inform itself well upon matters of such deep importance, and prepare to decide upon the course best calculated to produce the greatest benefit that England can derive from her connexion with India, and in return, to secure to our Indian subjects the utmost benefit they can reap from their connexion with Great Britain. That such an opinion as that just alluded to should exist in this enlightened age, is a lamentable illustration of the existence of an ignorance which it is difficult to imagine. Our author, in continuation, observes, "The possession of British India has contributed mainly to augment the resources of England, and to give it weight and influence amongst the nations of Europe." If this remark be true, and apparently it is correct, it would naturally lead to the consideration of a very serious question — Whether England, in the present changed condition of things, could maintain her exalted position amongst the nations of the world if stripped of her Indian possessions? If it be granted that India is of such material importance, it is self-evident that her importance principally rests upon the benefits to be derived from commercial intercourse with her; and if she be the ventricle which supplies our country with the blood of life, we are bound, as we value our existence, to act upon the necessity of self-preservation, minutely to examine every part of our commercial policy, and make such changes as will render our trade beneficial in the highest degree it is capable of proving to both countries.

If the charge of unfitness brought against the Company, as an organ through which our traffic to the East is to be carried on, by the author of "Colonial Policy" be true, it is manifest the continuation of its exclusive privileges must prove highly injurious to the rights of the community, and consequently at variance with the true interests of the nation. If a free trade would increase the imports of England and India, and if the gain of a nation depends upon its imports, as all political writers tell us, they must mutually suffer from restrictions which necessarily become impolitic, and should be removed. Experience has proved the genius of monopolies to tend to the contraction and perversion of the laws of nature. They confine the copious and bountiful stream intended by Providence for the general good of mankind, within the narrow limits prescribed by the selfish and aggrandizing spirit of corporations, through the medium of an apathetic legislature. If, upon the expiration of the present charter, the blessings of a free trade be given to India, she will, in some measure, be compensated for all the wrongs and injuries she has endured. The British nation, too, will largely participate in the good effects consequent on the throwing open of our Eastern commerce. Competition will be attended by a fall in price, which will naturally lead to increased consumption, and thereby enable us to revise and decrease our excise and custom duties without sustaining loss of revenue. The comforts and conveniences of life will then spread widely amongst an improved and grateful people.

Our possessions in the East Indies, although not really colonial, should, with respect to foreign nations, be considered as strictly so, and all communication with them be conducted upon similar principles. We should then become the carriers of

Europe for India, by which our customs and marine establishment would be infinitely increased. All national restrictions should be done away, and international ones imposed;—this would render England in a great measure independent of the commerce of Europe, the nations of which would be compelled to purchase from her, and she would naturally become the medium through which the commerce of the continental nations passed to the East, and *vice versa*. Her fleets and merchants would thus spread over the world; and, as she is the acknowledged mistress of the ocean, so she would become the emporium of all civilized nations: the palpable advantage of which is fully illustrated by the flourishing condition of our trade with the East Indies during the war, and its present deteriorated state. All our possessions should trade freely with each other and the mother country, receiving, through her, the produce of foreign states for internal consumption.

Few things can exceed in magnitude or importance the manner in which the national commerce is regulated; for upon it the power and character of the nation depends. As it affects Great Britain and its dependencies, there cannot be a more interesting or a more serious question. From the time of Lord Bacon down to the present day, we have been told that monopolies and exclusive companies, although necessary to trade carried on with barbarous nations, are pernicious, in the highest degree, to the true interests of commercial intercourse. Nothing can be more wantonly extravagant, nor more cruelly unjust, than commercial restrictions and heavy duties. They impoverish and stunt the natural energies and enterprise of the nation in their very source. They undermine alike the industry and morals of the people; and whilst they impede the progress of the public in the acquisition of comfort, distinction and wealth, they foster and forward the natural tendencies inherent in us to every species of crime that can degrade and pollute the mind. Let the restrictions upon our commerce be removed, our excise laws revised, and the duties on trade be diminished: our revenues will then be secured; smuggling and illicit trade, with their attendant enormities, will be banished from the land. Nothing can be more pernicious than the manner in which our trade with India is carried on; the system is alike injurious and intolerable, and at once shamefully and gratuitously lavish of the rights of the public. If that which contributes most to the improvement of the human mind, and thence to the condition of society, be unquestionably that which calls for the most thorough investigation, and as commerce has been traced and proved to be the great source from which intellect and wealth, the foundation of all national glory, flow, it is obviously that to which we should look with the greatest anxiety and most scrupulous solicitude.

MILITARY.

"It is not difficult to discover, that the present exalted situation of our Indian possessions has much less to hope than to fear from the chance of arms; that in the prosecution of remote wars, the undertaking gradually becomes more difficult, the event more doubtful, the possession more precarious and less beneficial. The present character of our arms will add weight to the dignity of moderation, and we may preserve peace by a constant state of preparation for war." Whilst we regulate our conduct by the principle of justice, we must shew to the nations upon our confines, that we are as little disposed to endure as to offer an injury. Under the influence of this principle we should look to the present condition of our army.

In contemplating the military branch of the present system, we should never forget that the British dominions in India have been achieved by our native army in conjunction with a very small European force, and that our sovereignty must be upheld by that army; it consequently follows, that the honour, comfort, and independence of the officers and men of which it is composed, are the principal, if not the sole means, by which its fidelity and devotion can be preserved ; and that these essentials, once tainted, the transition to discontent and indifference, and a conviction of having suffered wrong and of having been treated with ingratitude, is a natural and not improbable result. That such a disposition, or even a tendency to it, would be quickly discerned and taken advantage of by the native powers, requires no illustration ; but allowing, for the sake of argument, that it remained unheeded, the condition contains seeds within itself that must come, in the course of time, to a crisis, which could neither be averted by cajoling, nor removed by force. It matters little whether the officers or men, or both, are imbued with feelings that cannot but produce the most disastrous consequences, allowing even that they may not be attended by the immediate and utter annihilation of our dominion. Let us, therefore, a moment pause and dwell upon the former condition, and present state of our Indian army; and, as we examine the changes which have necessarily taken place, endeavour to trace their effects. Such a course of proceeding is indispensable, if we are anxious to correct defects.

History informs us, that at the commencement of our career, when our superiority, being new, operated most powerfully, its influence was without limit, and without opposition. That the seat of war in these early times was at the very doors of our soldiery, who were led by eminent commanders whom they idolized, and officered by distinguished men who were known, and beloved ; that both were associated with their interests, and glory, and participated alike in their dangers, fatigues, and privations. In times of peace their allowances were such as to enable them to lay by an independence, and in times of war ample for procuring every necessary and many comforts. Such was the condition of the men, and that of their officers was by no means less enviable. Present allowances ample, wealth and honors awaiting them, and an early return to their country with a wreath on their brow, and a fortune adequate to afford every rational enjoyment, was an object which cheered every man to exertion, and was not beyond the grasp of any who devoted their talents to their attainment. Let us now view the present condition of the army, and we thall see every thing reversed. Extended dominion naturally removes the soldiery further from home, fewer wars decrease the chance of advancement to rank, or independence, and increase in the opposite ratio the fatigue, and hardships of the field. The long continuance, too, of peace, at half batta stations,* deprives the soldier of the means of providing for the extra expense and

* There is not at present a single full batta station for our native soldiers on the Bengal establishment, and half batta ones are now established for our European officers, which has occasioned a feverish excitement throughout the army.

losses inseparable from a constant preparation for service, in which condition he must be; neither can it be concealed that Government was more scrupulously attentive to its native army in former times than it is at present. Troops going upon foreign service used to be provided, not with necessaries only, but with luxuries. At present no such attention is paid to their convenience or their wants.* In proof of this, let us look to some of the last volunteering detachments, and see how our troops were used at Ceylon under General *****, who made our Hindoos go to church, and tried to make them feed on salt provisions from our ships! Let us again look to our army that went to Java, and consider the terms upon which they went abroad, and the treatment they received, and we shall be constrained to acknowledge they were not well used. They went abroad under a promise, either given or implied, that their officers should not be removed from their corps; that they should, when the service was over, be immediately brought back. How was this pledge, that should have been considered sacred, and preserved inviolate, redeemed? Their officers were removed according to contingencies, and they were not relieved, when they might have been, nor so soon as they had reason to expect; the result of which was, they conceived their old officers to have been re-

* The conduct of the Madras Government, under the late Sir T. Munro, to the Madras troops in Ava, forms a happy contrast to that of the sister presidency.

moved for the purpose of clearing the way to their being kept upon the island altogether. This impression led naturally enough to the contrivance of means to effect their deliverance from what they considered banishment, which they viewed with feelings aggravated by their love of home, and religious prejudice. The most obvious road to the attainment of the inestimable object in view, in comparison with which life was below consideration, was joining the standard of the deposed Rajah, under a positive stipulation, that when they had restored him to his lost dominions, he should restore them to their native land. In such a compact the most microscopic eye cannot detect the slightest tendency to a spirit of turbulence or rebellion, and every act to which their feelings impelled them must in fairness be attributed rather to the temerity, and bad faith of Government, than to a violent and insubordinate disposition amongst themselves. Their intention was, however, happily discovered; the ringleaders were seized, tried for mutiny, condemned, and some of them executed. The next instance we shall notice shall be more recent, that it may come home to the feelings more than circumstances long past, perhaps scarcely known, or long since forgotten, can possibly do. Our Burman war, it is well known to every person, however slightly acquainted with Indian affairs, has been carried on under the severest trials and privations to which a soldier can be exposed. Some native troops stationed at Barrackpore were ordered to march to the theatre of war; a demand was made for the necessary aid, and not acquiesced with; obedience was peremptorily insisted upon; the troops remained sullen, and the dreadful catastrophe that followed is unhappily too generally known. They had no old officers with them, their colonel but just arrived from Europe, and previous to his joining them had long been employed upon the staff, and was of course a stranger. The other officers of the 47th were generally unknown to the men, in consequence of the many changes and removals attending the formation of the several battalions composing the army into regiments. At such a moment, and under such circumstances, would not the peculiarity of the exigency have warranted, if it did not imperatively demand, a minute and impartial investigation of a matter pregnant with present and future consequences of the last importance to our Eastern possessions? Were effectual means taken? If so, why not have published them, if they served to fix the brand of ingratitude and mutiny upon a refractory and licentious soldiery, that measures of such uncommon rigour might go forth into the world accompanied by some show of justice, and supported by some appearance of necessity? No such proceedings were ever published; nay, the Gazette of the following week announced to the world and the deeply injured army, the concession of what their slaughtered comrades had required. Is it possible to conceive an act of such inconsistent imbecility? If the regiment had required that which was improper, it should never have been conceded; on the other hand, if it demanded a right or a requisite, it should have been freely acquiesced in, and the unwise proceeding would never have taken place, which at present sullies the reputation of an army, to whose valor and devotion we owe the conquest of our splendid empire, and whose deeds and fame must go down to posterity commingled with the glory of our country, so long as its remembrance shall endure.

The recollection of such fatal precipitation must continue to operate as an antidote against that affection and loyalty which is the very corner-stone upon which the mighty fabric we have raised in the East must be upborne. That the Indian army is entitled to the gratitude of our country cannot be denied, when we contemplate the deeds it has largely contributed to achieve, in perpetuation of the triumph of the genius of England in that distant land, the conquest of which bade defiance to the proud ambition of the Assyrian, the Greek, and the Roman. It therefore behoves us to recollect that an army, whose character has recently been exposed to obloquy, may at some and possibly at no distant day, be called upon to defend our sway against the gigantic efforts of the Czar of Russia. The policy of Peter the Great, and Catharine the Second, still continues to influence the councils of Saint Petersburgh, and England may yet be compelled to meet her in hostile array on the plains of Persia, or the shores of the Caspian. That this ill-timed concession was viewed by the army at large rather as a right forcibly wrung from unfeeling masters, than as a generous boon freely given by a liberal Government, careful of the welfare, and anxiously solicitous as to the comfort of its servants, cannot be doubted. Such acts are these are quite enough to force a conviction upon the most sceptical mind, of the necessity of some radical change in the system by which the army is regulated and conducted. Let us see how the European part of it fare. For the perfect comprehension of its actual condition, it will be indispensable that we advert to its former situation, with reference to that of His Majesty's army serving in India. In former times the number of European officers in the army was comparatively few; and although their promotion was slow, they enjoyed the substantial equivalent of handsome allowances from the time they entered the service, neither was there any obstacle to their attaining the highest rank to which it was possible to arrive in the Company's service. At present the officers are trebled, their pay, allowances, and the advantages of staff situations reduced to a mere sufficiency for their necessities, — an insurmountable bar to their rise in the service established, and every avenue leading to the hope of being ultimately able, should they even survive the vicissitudes of an Indian climate and the common accidents of life for half a century, to visit their native land in time to drop into the grave, essentially removed far beyond the reach of the most ardent spirit, and sanguine expectation.

Let us view the career of two young men proceeding at the same time to India, one an ensign in His Majesty's army, the other a cadet in the Honorable Company's service. The former of these can obtain the rank of a lieutenant-colonel in eight years, and that, too, by various means, either in the natural course of promotion, by purchase, family interest, or by brevet, which last includes three several roads to that rank, and two out of three even reach the rank of full colonel. Brevet is given for achievements in the field, so that it is not only possible, but sometimes occurs, that these young men commence their first campaign together. In the same field, within a few hundred yards of each other, they are both favored by fortune, and perform deeds which attract the notice of their commander-in-chief. One is rewarded by promotion to a lieutenancy, the other to a petty staff situation, such as the adjutancy of his regiment, when vacant, or a sub-assistant on the general staff. They again meet in the field under the partial influence of fortune, and are again distinguished above their associates in arms. Promotion to a company rewards the lieutenant; the ensign stands fast; he cannot be placed over the heads of those above him in the department; barren praise is his obvious and sole reward; he is however yet young, with a buoyant spirit, and a vigorous constitution, which is sufficient to support the lofty aspirations of a noble mind. He again enters the lists, borne on the wings of hope, and impelled by emulation, and again meets his early but more fortunate companion in arms, and is again with him advanced in fame. A brevet majority and companionship of the Bath is the merited reward of His Majesty's officer, whilst his no less meritorious comrade continues stationary, or is possibly advanced in the regular course of promotion to a lieutenancy. The advance of the former is accelerated by the claims he derives from the honors he has achieved, and his nomination to a deputy adjutant-generalship, or of a deputy quarter-master-general, gives him the anxiously sought rank of lieutenant-colonel. He may then get the command of a regiment at home, and enjoy, in the spring and prime of life, independence in his native land, amidst his kindred and his friends, and look forward to reaching, in the summer of his days, the elevated and enviable rank of a general officer, by which period his early friend has reached, after a distinguished and honorable service of thirty years, the rank of a lieutenant-colonel; about which period another fortunate officer in His Majesty's army, who has served eight years, arrives upon the same day at the rank to which the Company's veteran soldier has just risen. What is the result that may now occur, and what is the result that must inevitably take place? The former is His Majesty's officer, and may, either by interest or a glorious chance, be promoted to be an aide-de-camp to His Majesty, which gives him the permanent rank of colonel at once. What is now the second inevitable occurrence? Why, both officers being promoted to lieutenant-colonels' commissions on the same day, His Majesty's officer must take the precedence of the Company's whenever a brevet may be issued by the Crown, notwithstanding the latter arrived at his lieutenant-colonelcy in thirty, and the former in eight years. Here even this paralyzing supercession does not cease, but with a steady and undeviating step pursues its victim till the scene is closed by a shattered constitution, superannuation, and a broken spirit, in which condition he is driven from an ungrateful service in a foreign land, to his native country, where, when he arrives, he will be an isolated being, without rank, and without fortune, full of years, and weighed down by misery. Let us see for a moment the situation of His Majesty's soldier, who retires from the active duties of his profession, for the purpose of enjoying in tranquillity the remaining years of his life. His name, although he may be out of the army, continues in the list, and he retains by courtesy the rank he obtained in the service, and is received accordingly at the court of his own sovereign, as also at every court in Europe. But as if this long string of irreparable grievances was insufficient for the Company's officer, he is, whilst he continues in the performance of the duties of his profession, exposed to every degradation that supercession and a naturally partial commander can heap upon him. In illustration of which, let us refer to the two most recent occasions—the Burmese war, and the siege of Bhurtpore,—and it will be found that the complaint herein made rests upon a foundation that is not to be shaken. An assertion may be refuted, but a fact is irrefragable. Who were the commandants of the divisions under Colonel Sir A. Campbell? They were generally officers of His Majesty's army. If this be termed an unjust and a cruel partiality, and it be asked why such undue favor was shewn to the officers of one service in prejudice to the rights of those of the other, it may be replied that there was no officer of rank in the Indian army present in the country, to whose talents, experience, energy, physical capacity, and character, such an important trust and arduous undertaking could have been confided, with any reasonable expectation, that the result would prove triumphant. Such a preposterous and unjustifiable reason could not be brought forward, as General Sir John Doveton, of the Madras army, was upon the spot; and the qualities of this distinguished officer of known talents, energy, experience, physical capacity, and knowledge of the character of the elements of which the army was composed, pointed him out as an individual eminently conspicuous and qualified to lead our arms to conquest in a foreign land. But, alas! he was unfit, and rendered so by the commission which he bore; he was a Company's officer, and that alone was sufficient. It therefore followed as a matter of course that as the chief was, so must his aids be of the royal army. With the merits or conduct of the war we have no business in this place; our object is to draw the consideration of the public authorities to the degraded condition of the Indian army. Let us now turn to Bhurtpore, and we shall find a system of favoritism as unworthy, unjust, and pernicious in its chilling effects upon the hopes and energies of the Indian army, as that we have just left. Two king's major-generals were selected to command, under the commander-in-chief; could there have been a Company's general selected of sufficient talent to entitle him to a command? To this cruel and galling query we can answer in the affirmative. General Sir Gabriel Martindell was on the spot, and commanded at Cawnpore at the time that General Nichol was brought from Calcutta, a distance of one thousand miles. If this is not sufficient, let the treatment which that distinguished and celebrated veteran, Colonel Adams, experienced, speak the rest. He was in command of the citadel, with native troops; precautionary means had been adopted by him; the peace, lives, and properties of the people, as well as the honor of the British arms, were secure under his vigilance. The distinction of such a command was deemed beyond the deserts of the colonel and his gallant band. His Majesty's 14th Foot, under Colonel M'Combe, (a junior colonel too) was selected; they marched in, with colours flying, the morning after the place had been taken. The natives under Colonel Adams marched out; the citadel and part of the city was partially plundered. Such acts require no comment; the most culpable indifference is seldom blind to its own interests; and as those of the public are inseparable from the rights and honor of the Indian army, it is to be expected that the natural desire to preserve the one, will lead to the protection of the other. It is manifest our possessions were won by the valour and devotion of the army, and by it alone can our dominion be retained. Let it be divided, let dissensions be sown between it and His Majesty's army, and our empire will soon pass into other hands, or the numerous nations over whose destinies the genius of Great Britain presides, may be roused into action, and stimulated by the discord observed to reign throughout our army,—be induced to make a desperate struggle to regain an independence, the loss of which they have never ceased to mourn, and for the attainment of which they will never allow a favorable opportunity for making the attempt to pass by unheeded. The time therefore may arrive, and is probably not far distant, when the English nation (unless some remedy be soon applied to the existing evils) may be compelled to lament in the bitterness of unavailing repentance, its unaccountable apathy, and infatuated indifference to the unwise and invidious distinctions introduced into an army, upon whose unanimity and devotion it can alone repose in security.

In calling the notice of the public to this vitally important question, we shall insert in this place a short extract from the speech of Colonel Cathcart, in the debate upon Mr. Chancellor Pitt's Bill in 1784, which every way merits the mature consideration of the statesmen, who preside over the councils which regulate the government of our Indian possessions. That able officer justly remarks, "Either, Sir, motives of humanity are to induce us to restore to the natives of India those territories which from avarice or ambition we have wrested from them, or motives of policy are to predominate, and we are to attempt by arms to preserve those distant provinces. What, Sir, upon this latter supposition, can be of more immediate consequence than the regulation of those armies which we must maintain, to secure the fidelity of many millions of subjects, whose hearts, God knows, have no reason to be impressed with gratitude for favours already received under our government?

"Or, what, Sir, calls more loudly for the exercise of our humanity, than the consideration of what comforts we can point out for those soldiers who have embarked for that distant part of the world, in what it was their duty to consider their king's and country's cause? While we talk here of zeal for the welfare of the state, they have proved theirs by the sweat of their brows, and with their blood."

Our Indian army can never continue in its present state; it must either improve or deteriorate. It is now destitute of officers of rank, and will very shortly have nothing but old officers in subaltern situations in its ranks. At present even, we are under the necessity of bringing lieutenant-colonel commandants into situations that should be filled by major-generals, in the possession of both mental and physical capacity. It is really melancholy to observe the systematic indifference with which the interests of our Indian army are treated; neglect is fast eradicating every sentiment that should be cultivated in a soldier's mind, and every desire that should be cherished in his heart, — the love of fame, the desire of distinction, gratitude to his employers, and devotion to their service; without these he will dwindle into a mere mercenary, and prove but a broken reed in the hour of danger. It is obvious, then, that the Indian army must either be reorganized or transferred to the crown, and which of these alterations is to be pursued should be examined with a deliberate, patient and unprejudiced judgment.

In arranging for the improvement of the European officers of our army, the situation of our native officers should not be passed over. We should profit by the example we have before us in the French army previous to the revolution, in which the gentry of the land were debarred rising to rank, emolument and command. The European portion of our Indian armies may be, in some measure, likened to the noblesse of the old French armies; and assuredly the day will come, unless timely provision be made, when the native gentry of India and the subordinate native soldiers of our Indian army, will avail themselves of an opportunity to acquire by force, rights in which our policy denies them participation.

We shall conclude this part of our subject by recommending to the consideration of those whose duty it is to watch over our Indian interests, the maxim said in Montesquieu's Persian Letters to have existed in France in his time. "We have a maxim in France," replied he, "never to promote officers whose patience hath languished in subaltern offices; we regard them as persons whose understandings are straitened by a narrow sphere of action, and who, accustomed to little things, are become incapable of greater."

Never was there a wiser maxim, nor can there be a more obvious reason for accelerating promotion instead of thwarting it, as we do in our Indian army. We should court its affections, and conciliate its feelings, rather than alienate the one and violate the other, as is done every day by supercession and neglect.

The foregoing sheets were ready for the press before we happened to take up the 70th Number of the Quarterly Review, in which, to our astonishment, we read as follows, in page 490.

"That the Sepoy officers and soldiers were afraid of the Burman, there cannot be the smallest doubt; and, indeed, throughout the campaign they never could be safely trusted to lead in an attack, although, in defending a post, they always behaved well. In the defence of Kemmendine they deserved great credit for their steady behaviour; but in the attack of the stockades on the 15th December, after their retreat from before Rangoon, when ordered to the assault, the whole battalion actually laid themselves down, and the British troops marched to the assault over them." Again, in the same page, we find the following: — "Colonel Smith was ordered on an expedition a few miles from Rangoon, and from his high opinion of the Native troops, he requested that they alone might be employed in the enterprize. Sir Archibald Campbell indulged him, and the consequence was, that the Burmans, seeing there were no white faces, fought most courageously, and the Sepoys, unable to stand the assault, were panic struck and totally defeated." In page 500 we find stated, "We have strong grounds for believing that the unfortunate business at Barrackpore was, in a great degree, owing to the superstitious dread of the Burmese and their charms, nay, that this idea was not confined to the regiments then and there present, but at the time pervaded the Native soldiery to a very extraordinary extent. Yet these are the troops to whom we mainly owe, and by whom we hold an empire over seventy or eighty millions of people."

We fairly put it to the public. Is it probable that such an act of pusillanimity as is above asserted as a fact, could have occurred in the face of an army and escape observation? Is it probable that, being known, it would have been kept concealed? Is it probable that a public staff-officer, in the family of the commander-in-chief, his assistant in the political department, in detailing the proceedings of the army, in which an act, casting indelible disgrace upon the service, occurred, would have been silent upon it, or dared to refrain from expressing the indignation felt by the whole of the troops at such dastardly and ignominious conduct, feeling, as he must have felt, had it taken place, that concealment, in some cases, is as gross a dereliction of the duty of a narrator, as falsely asserting that which he knew to be untrue? Is it probable that a general officer, commanding an army in which a circumstance, pregnant with the utmost danger, threatening even the existence of the state, would presume to keep government in ignorance of that which it deeply concerned it to know, and which it was his paramount duty to report? Or is it probable that government, upon being made acquainted with an act which must necessarily have shaken the confidence hitherto placed in an army whose reputation for zeal and courage had never been questioned, would have connived at its own ultimate annihilation, by abstaining from visiting with exemplary severity a cowardly and debased body which had abandoned every claim to consideration, and rendered itself obnoxious to disgrace and punishment? With so many concurring improbabilities opposed to the Quarterly Reviewer's *fact*, we shall leave it to its fate.

The next incident, Colonel Smith's having requested native troops alone to be sent on an expedition a few miles from Rangoon, is given on authority that may "be relied on," in a manner so totally different from the dispatches as published by government, as to render any elaborate notice of it in this place worse than useless. If we are not mistaken, the expedition a few miles from Rangoon was at a distance that occupied a march of twelve hours, the road, for the most part of the way, lying under water; that the enemy, in numbers, were found in a fortified position, and that Colonel Smith's detachment was unfurnished with guns, ladders, or any necessary for an escalade; and that, instead of a few miles, and in a known spot, the enemy was found at so great a distance, that the troops must have been exhausted by their fatiguing and distressing march before they were exposed to the enemy's fire from behind inaccessible stockades. Is the disastrous result of this expedition, or the successful one of the next day, composed entirely of Europeans, equipped with guns and ladders, a matter of astonishment, or a fit occasion for decrying the failure of an expedition which it was morally impossible could succeed under the circumstances of the case? This was, we believe, the second time the native troops had been detached by themselves, and without guns or ladders, to dispossess Burmese troops in positions strongly fortified.* Sending

* See the account of Colonel M'Dowell's expedition.

troops on a service in which defeat is nearly certain, would appear an admirable method of depriving them of confidence in themselves, and inspiring "a more than superstitious dread" of the result of attacks which it must have been evident could not succeed. We need not say any thing more upon Colonel Smith's affair. Let the authority that "may be relied on" be produced, until which time the public will pause before it yields credence to mere assertion.

We now come to the last charge brought forward upon "strong grounds," not indeed against any particular body, nor any particular presidency, but an unqualified accusation against the whole "native soldiery," and a more heartless libel never issued from the press.

The affair at Barrackpore had better not have been alluded to. It is wise to abstain from agitating circumstances that cannot but produce evil consequences; and (to use the words of the late Mr. Huskisson) "not to descend into the arena where honour is not to be won, and where to be vanquished would be disgrace indeed." It behoves those who have had any active concern in participating the tragic event, so cruelly and unjustifiably perverted, to check the folly that would force a discussion, fatal in its effects to the characters of more than those who fell in that calamitous catastrophe. We shall take our leave of this accusation with the remark, that an enquiry into the cause of the occurrences of that fatal day was instituted. Let the proceedings be given to the world, and if the memory of those who paid the penalty of their crime, with their lives, deserves the opprobrium so lavishly poured upon them and their brethren in arms, we shall retire with sorrow and humiliation from a cause justly meriting the brand of eternal disgrace.

We now come to the climax so exultingly put forth, "Yet these are the troops to whom we mainly owe, and by whom we hold an empire over seventy or eighty millions of people!" We can only reply, Yes, they are the troops, by whom England won, and with whom she must maintain her mighty dominion over seventy or eighty millions of people! Let the above exclamation, issued in the imagined triumph of arrogance, emanate from whence it may, it can only be viewed as a puerile attempt to traduce the reputation of those, who, as soldiers and men, are beyond their imitation, and above their reproach.

It is but lost labour to attack the unsullied honor and gallantry of the native soldiery; for the descendants of men who followed a Clive, a Lawrence, a Coote, a Cornwallis, a Lake, and a Wellington, contemn scurrilous abuse, and may fairly challenge the admiration of all whose applause is worth a soldier's ambition.

Yes, these are the troops who followed those renowned captains with a spirit upon which they could and did rely; and their descendants of the present day, would follow with unabated ardour, and undeteriorated qualities, any commander who understood their character, respected their prejudices, or regarded their affections.

But let Government, under the fatal spell of infatuation, select officers to command them, whose characters are different from those of the great men, the recollection of whose fostering care, personal worth, and splendid deeds, is fondly cherished by a grateful and admiring posterity; and England may yet have to chaunt a requiem over the departure of that affection to which she owes her dominion in the East.

Sensible of the difficulty of restraining the expression of feelings wantonly violated, we would willingly obey the dictates of a natural repugnance to refute party writers; but when the misrepresentation of a meritorious and highly distinguished body, whose services and blood have raised a proud monument to our country's glory in a distant land, is abruptly forced upon us, we cannot refrain from expressing our abhorrence of such aspersions.

THE END.